Monographic Journals of the Near East

T0153649

...asiatic Linguistics 7/4 (May 1980)

PARADIGM COHERENCE: EVIDENCE FROM MODERN HEBREW

by

Shmuel Bolozky
University of Massachusetts

Data from Modern Hebrew support the principle of paradigm coherence and the claim that inflection tends to minimize allomorphy while derivation preserves it. It is shown, however, that analogical change is a function of the degree of automaticity of the morphological and syntactic relationships concerned, and thus close inter-paradigmatic alternations may be subject to analogy as well. The direction of analogy can be determined either by reference to the unmarked base form or to opacity considerations.

CONTENTS

1. INTRODUCTION

Paradigm coherence, i.e. loss of alternation resulting in a more uniform paradigm, and the role it plays in phonological description, have recently been discussed quite extensively in generative phonology: see, for instance, King (1969, 1972), Kiparsky (1971, 1972), Wanner (1972), Vennemann (1972 a,b; 1974 a,b), Harris (1973), Miller (1973), Skousen (1975), de Chene (1975), Hooper (1976). The main proponents of the incorporation of the principle of paradigm coherence in generative phonology have been Kiparsky and Vennemann, who demonstrated that it would be quite difficult to account for certain phenomena unless they are explained by leveling due to paradigm coherence. The independence of the principle of paradigm coherence has been challenged, and it was acknowledged in Kiparsky (1974) that although it cannot always be motivated by simplicity considerations, it at least normally *results* in a simpler system. Kiparsky (1974) *cautiously* defends paradigm coherence as an independently motivated linguistic principle, then.

The phenomenon of minimization of allomorphy in inflectional paradigms is illustrated in this paper with data from Modern Hebrew, and it is reasserted that the typical distribution of leveled and unleveled forms is indeed such that leveling applies in inflections, whereas derivations tend to preserve allomorphy (Kiparsky 1972). The Hebrew data suggest, however, that for the purpose of leveling, the boundaries between inflection and derivation are not clear-cut and that there exist borderline derivational relationships which in some respects are inflectional in character. In fact, one could speak of a continuum, in which syntactic and morphological relationships are strongest in a tense paradigm within a certain inflection, are somewhat less strong in the verbal conjugation as a whole, diminish somewhat between a verbal conjugation and its infinitive, decrease further between a conjugation and its derived nominalization and somewhat further between a conjugation and its passive verbal counterpart, and so on. Analogy (here used to cover both paradigmatic leveling and inter-paradigmatic analogical extension) decreases as the syntactic and morphological bond weakens; the degree of weakening of these syntactic and morphological relations is often reflected in decreased capability to automatically predict the occurrence of alternating forms from each other. Thus, the likelihood of analogy depends on the strength of the intra-paradigmatic or inter-paradigmatic relationship between alternating forms, measured by the extent to which, given a certain form, one can predict that its alternant will form an actual word, i.e. would not constitute a lexical gap, and what its meaning is going to be. Within an inflectional paradigm, and particularly in a tense paradigm within an inflectional paradigm, the occurrence of one form presupposes the existence of all other members of the paradigm. The same is true of the relationship between a finite verbal form and its infinitival realization. The relationship between a finite verbal form and its direct nominalization is also quite automatic, though not as automatic as its relationship with the corresponding infinitive: some verbs cannot be nominalized; sometimes there is an unexplainable gap and in the absence of a gerundial form related to one paradigm, another gerund is used, usually associated with a different paradigm; and so on. Given a form in a transitive paradigm, its passive counterpart can be derived fairly automatically—though again, not as automatically as nominalizations are from their corresponding verbal forms. Given a form in one inflectional paradigm, deriving its counterpart in another paradigm that is not passive is much less automatic—many roots realized in one conjugation cannot be realized in another; others *are* realized in the other conjugation, but acquire a totally unrelated meaning. The relationship between a verbal form and any non-verbal form that does not constitute an immediate nominalization is much less productive: derivational productivity there is often restricted to a set of morphemes that must be marked in the lexicon for undergoing the derivation in question. It will be shown below that the likelihood of analogy diminishes with this gradual decrease in automaticity of derivation, which reflects the weakening of syntactic and morphological relations from "true" inflection to "true" derivation. No stand is taken as to whether automatic relationship should imply unique underlying representation; the argument in Barkai (1975) that, in Hebrew, unique underlying representations should only be assumed for paradigm-internal surface alternation, is not necessarily challenged. Although the primary evidence for such an argument is probably the predominance of leveling within inflection, the occurrence of analogy in (automatic) derivations as well is not introduced as counter-evidence, though it might be interpreted as such. Analogy is investigated independently of the question of uniqueness of underlying representations.

Automaticity is not claimed to be a sufficient condition for analogy. Alternants in an automatic relationship are seldom leveled when there still exists a transparent (Kiparsky 1971, 1973) phonological process capturing the alternation concerned. In other words, for an alternation to be leveled, the rule capturing this alternation should be sufficiently opaque, i.e. contradicted on the surface, to allow leveling. That there might be a correlation between opacity and leveling was already pointed out in King (1972) and was also implied in Vennemann (1972a). Vennemann shows that when rule loss is due to paradigm coherence, it is usually preceded by the addition of another rule obscuring the phonetic motivation of the original rule (1972a:188).

Concerning directionality of leveling, i.e. whether leveling is with the input of the original rule or with its output, it is shown that as suggested in Vennemann (1974a), speakers tend to level with the unmarked base form. When analogy is not with the unmarked form, the explanations suggested are based on the nature of opacity involved and on avoidance of semantic ambiguity (cf. also Kiparsky (1972), Bolozky (1977), Barkai (1978)). Thus, opacity resulting from inapplication of the original rule (or from what is interpreted as inapplication), even though the structural description is met (Kiparsky's (1971) case i), would usually cause analogy with the input, since the speaker is no longer sure whether the rule should indeed be applied where it is supposed to apply. On the other hand, when opacity results from overapplication of the rule (or from what may be interpreted as overapplication) in the wrong environment (Kiparsky's (1971) case ii), analogy would normally follow the output, since the speaker would tend to overgeneralize a phonetic change that exists anyway if he finds surface support for doing so. Also, analogy would generally not yield forms whose formation would create semantic ambiguity, and obviously would not allow violating constraints on surface sequences.

2. SPIRANTIZATION

Biblical Hebrew stops were spirantized postvocalically. In Modern Hebrew, spirantization is restricted to $p \sim f$, $b \sim v$ and $k \sim x$, and has been widely morphologized. It needs to be reformulated with a few sub-parts, and even then exceptions abound.

Below are some possible reformulations of spirantization in sub-parts, as manifest in some groups of alternating forms (stress falls on the final vowel, unless marked otherwise).

2.1. Word-final spirantization

Spirantization applies word-finally, in a group of words that are lexically marked for undergoing it, as in (1):

(1)	**Plural**	**Singular**	**Gloss**
	rakim	*rax*	'soft' (masc.)
	zakim	*zax*	'pure' (masc.)
	masakim	*masax*	'screen'
	musakim	*musax*	'garage'

panakim	*panax*	'mess tin'
rabim	*rav*	'considerable' (masc.)
sabim	*sav*	'turn' (pres. masc.)
cabim	*cav*	'tortoise'
gabot	*gav*	'back'
dubim	*dov*	'bear' (masc.)
ceubim	*caov*	'yellow' (masc.)
retubim	*ratov*	'wet'
dapim	*daf*	'page'
kapot	*kaf*	'spoon'
apim	*af*	'nose'
tupim	*tof*	'drum'
sipim	*saf*	'porch, threshold'

Alternations as in (1) exist only in a restricted group of morphemes. Non-alternating forms as in (2)

(2)	**Plural**	**Singular**	**Gloss**
	bruxim	*barux*	'blessed' (masc.)
	šovaxim	*šovax*	'pigeon coop'
	kuxim	*kux*	'niche'
	tovim	*tov*	'good'
	oyvim	*oyev*	'enemy'
	šovavim	*šovav*	'naughty' (masc.)
	xofim	*xof*	'coast'
	nofim	*nof*	'landscape'
	ofot	*of*	'fowl, chicken'

are numerous, and certainly outnumber the alternating ones.

Here, leveling is from stop to spirant only. In singular-plural pairs the singular is the unmarked form, and since the singular always contains a spirant, one would expect leveling from stop to spirant. A partial reason might be avoidance of homonymity, e.g. *rak* 'only' from historical /raq/ should be distinguished from *rax* 'soft'.

Since leveling is these cases is only from stop to spirant, *masakim, musakim* and *panakim* seem to have turned into *masaxim, musaxim* and *panaxim* respectively as soon as they were used colloquially; *savim, cavim* and *retuvim* are the colloquial counterparts of *sabim, cabim* and *retubim* respectively, which are hardly ever used; and *afim, ceuvim* are sometimes heard in sub-standard or child speech. The preference for spirants in forms like *masaxim, musaxim, panaxim, savim, cavim* and *retuvim,* which must have been in existence for some time now, seems to suggest that restructuring took place, and that leveling with the spirant should synchronically be considered leveling with the *input.*

Non-automatic derivations are never analogized. In *rav* 'considerable' ~ *harbe* 'a lot', *sav* 'he turned' ~ *mesiba* 'party', one never hears **harve* or **mesiva* respectively. On the other hand, if the derivation is more regular, as in formation of *i*-final adjectives, etc. in (3), analogy may be possible, though marginal.

(3)	Noun	Derived Form	Alternative Pronunciation
	cav 'tortoise'	*cabi* 'tortoise-like'	*cavi*
	af 'nose'	*api* 'nasal'	*afi*
	af 'nose'	*meanpef* 'have nasal speech'	*meanfef*
	tof 'drum'	*tipuf* 'drumming'	*tifuf*

The last example in (3) is a case of almost obligatory leveling, but that may be due to the fact that throughout the related verbal paradigm, *f* is never realized as *p* (*tofef* 'he drummed' ~ *metofef* 'he drums' ~ *yetofef* 'he will drum').

2.2   Spirantization stem-initially after a vowel

Another sub-rule of spirantization applies stem-initally after a vowel (cf. Barkai 1975), as illustrated in (4) below:

(4)	Conjugation	Past 3rd Pers. Masc. Sing.	Present Masc. Sing.	Fut. 3rd Pers. Masc. Sing.	Imperative Masc. Sing.	Gloss
	pa'al	*patax*	*potéax*	*yiftax*	*ptax*	'open'
		pašat	*pošet*	*yifšot*	*pšot*	'take off'
		pakad	*poked*	*yifkod*	*pkod*	'order'
		badak	*bodek*	*yivdok*	*bdok*	'check'
		barax	*boreax*	*yivrax*	*brax*	'escape'
		bagad	*boged*	*yivgod*	*bgod*	'betray'
		katav	*kotev*	*yixtov*	*ktov*	'write'
		kavaš	*koveš*	*yixboš*	*kvoš*	'conquer'
		kav'av	*ko'ev*	*yix'av*	*(k'av)*	'hurt' (intr.)
	pi'el	*piter*	*mefater*	*yefater*	*pater*	'fire, dismiss'
		pitéax	*mefatéax*	*yefatéax*	*patéax*	'develop'
		pišet	*mefašet*	*yefašet*	*pašet*	'simplify'
		bitel	*mevatel*	*yevatel*	*batel*	'cancel'
		biser	*mevaser*	*yevaser*	*baser*	'bring news'
		bikeš	*mevakeš*	*yevakeš*	*bakeš*	'ask'
		kibed	*mexabed*	*yexabed*	*kabed*	'respect'
		kiven	*mexaven*	*yexaven*	*kaven*	'aim'
		kibes	*mexabes*	*yexabes*	*kabes*	'launder'

Pu'al cases are not specifed here. They are all passive counterparts of the above *pi'el* cases; the only differences are that the *-i-e-* and *-a-e-* vowel patterns are replaced by *-u-a-*, and that *pu?al* has no imperative.

Spirantization in (4) is paradigm-internal, within inflections, and as expected, the alternations concerned would be subject to leveling. The rule is also sufficiently opaque to allow leveling. In Ben-Horin and Bolozky (1972), three major degrees of opacity were distinguished for Spirantization. It was argued that the $k \sim x$ part is the most opaque, since both the input and output can be confused with historically distinct segments that are no longer distinguishable as independent phonemes: /q/ has merged with *k* and /ħ/ with *x*; the $b \sim v$ part is less opaque, since only the output can be confused: Biblical /w/ has merged with *v*; and the $p \sim f$ part is the least oqaque, since neither input nor output can be confused. This last observation, concerning $p \sim f$, is only partly correct, since one finds numerous borrowed verbs (mostly colloquial) with initial *f*, and this *f* is hardly ever realized as *p*, as can be seen in (5):

(5)	Past 3rd Pers. Masc. Sing.	Present Masc. Sing.	Fut. 3rd Pers. Masc. Sing.	Imperative Masc. Sing.	Gloss
	fibrek	*mefabrek*	*yefabrek*	*fabrek*	'fabricate'
	flirtet	*meflartet*	*yeflartet*	*flartet*	'flirt'
	filéax	*mefaléax*	*yefaléax*	*faléax*	'steal'
	fisfes	*mefasfes*	*yefasfes*	*fasfes*	'miss'

Since in native Hebrew, stops and corresponding spirants are supposed to be in complementary distribution, the output of spirantization seems to show up where spirantization should not have applied, i.e. spirantization is made opaque by what looks like overapplication, at least according to Kiparsky (1971). It should not be opaque according to Kiparsky (1973), since the spirants in initial position do not arise by spirantization. For the same reason, ex-/w/and ex-/ħ/ would not cause opacity either. However, since the stops and the spirants in question were in complementary distribution, and speakers have associated initial position with the stops, I believe that word-initial *x* from /ħ/, *v* from /w/ and borrowed *f* were and still are the primary reason for spirantization becoming increasingly opaque, just as *k* from /q/ is. As there are hardly any borrowed verbs with stem-initial postvocalic *p*, borrowing does not add exceptions involving inapplication to the $p \sim f$ part, i.e. no case (i) opacity and no leveling by the input. There are some borrowed verbs with initial *b* that is not spirantized in postvocalic stem-initial position, as in (6):

(6)	Past 3rd Pers. Masc. Sing.	Present Masc. Sing.	Fut. 3rd Pers. Masc. Sing.	Imperative Masc. Sing.	Gloss
	bilef	*mebalef*	*yebalef*	*balef*	'lie, bluff'

but their number is very small. Essentially, then, both the $b \sim v$ and $p \sim f$ parts of spirantization are made opaque by what looks like overapplication, whereas the opacity of the $k \sim x$ part is caused by what looks like both inapplication and overapplication, since ex-/q/ and ex-/ħ/ often occur in stem-initial postvocalic position.

As expected from the nature of opacity involved, then, $k \sim x$ alternations within inflections would undergo leveling both with the input and the output. The same pairs with $k \sim x$, $k \sim k$ or $x \sim x$ may be in free variation in sub-standard colloquial use, as in (7):

1980]	Paradigm Coherence in Hebrew	7

(7)	Past 3rd Pers. Masc. Sing.	Fut. 3rd Pers. Masc. Sing.	Imperative Masc. Sing.	Gloss
	kiven	yexaven	kaven	'aim'
or	kiven	yekaven	kaven	
or	xiven	yexaven	xaven	
	kibes	yexabes	kabes	'launder'
or	kibes	yekabes	kabes	
or	xibes	yexabes	xabes	
	kibed	yexabed	kabed	'respect'
or	kibed	yekabed	kabed	
or	xibed	yexabed	xabed	

Presumably, combinations such as *xiven ~ yekaven ~ xaven* could also result, but to the best of my knowledge are not as common.

Typically, the leveled pair is the sub-standard or marginally standard counterpart of the unleveled one, as in (8):

(8)	Past 3rd Pers. Masc. Sing.	Fut. 3rd Pers. Masc. Sing.	Imperative Masc. Sing.	Gloss
	katav	yixtov	ktov	'write'
or	katav	yiktov	ktov	
or	xatav	yixtov	xtov	
	kavaš	yixboš	kvoš	'conquer'
or	kavaš	yikboš/yikvoš	kvoš/kboš	
or	??xavaš	yixboš/yixvoš	xvoš/xboš	
	karat	yixrot	krot	'cut down'
or	karat	yikrot	krot	
or	??xarat	yixrot	xrot	
	kaʔav	yixʔav		'hurt' (int.)
or	kaʔav	yikʔav		
or	??xaʔav	yixʔav		

xatav, ??*xavaš* and ??*xarat* are found in child speech only. There is probably still a strong sense in which past, third person singular masculine *paʔal* forms are felt to be the basic, unmarked forms, and thus normally do not themselves undergo leveling in adult speech, even when colloquial. The marginality of ??*xavaš* and ??*xarat* is further increased by the existence of homonymous forms with *x* from ex-/ħ/: *xavaš* 'he bandaged' and *xarat* 'he engraved', respectively. Homonymity does not arise in the future and the imperative, since the counterparts of, say, *yixboš* and *xvoš* with *x* from /k/ are *yaxboš* and *xavoš* respectively when ex-/ħ/ is involved. It should be noted, however, that since this clue in *pa'al* future and imperative for the distinction between *x* from /ħ/ and *x* from /k/ is not found in *pi'el* (e.g. no distinction between *xišev ~yexašev ~xašev* 'compute', from ex-/ħ/, and *xiven ~yexaven ~xaven*, from /k/), it could explain why *pi'el*, which is semantically opaque in this respect, is still subject to leveling. Perhaps there happen to be no *actual* homonyms in *pi'el*. Regarding homonymity, however, it should be emphasized that avoidance of homonymity is only a *tendency*, since homonyms do exist (Bolozky (1977)).

b ~v alternations within inflections normally level with the output only, in spite of the input being the unmarked alternant. This is what the presence of apparent overapplication and absence of inapplication exceptions would predict. This, in (9) we find:

	(9)	Past 3rd Pers. Masc. Sing.	Fut. 3rd Pers. Masc. Sing.	Imperative Masc. Sing.	Gloss
		bikeš	*yevakeš*	*bakeš*	'ask'
or		*vikeš*	*yevakeš*	*vakeš*	
but not		*bikeš*	**yebakeš*	*bakeš*	
		berex	*yevarex*	*barex*	'congratulate'
or		*virex*	*yevarex*	*varex*	
but not		*berex*	**yebarex*	*barex*	
		bitel	*yevatel*	*batel*	'cancel'
or		*vitel*	*yevatel*	*vatel*	
but not		*bitel*	**yebatel*	*batel*	

Such leveling rarely occurs in *pa'al;* even children hardly ever realize *barax* as ?**varax*. Besides the above mentioned reason, that past third person singular masculine *pa'al* forms are still felt to be basic, there also happen to be no verbs starting with ex-/w/ in *pa'al*, i.e. there is no cause for *b ~v* opacity in *pa'al*. In *pi'el*, on the other hand, we do have such verbs, e.g. *viter* 'he gave up', *vide* 'he verified', *viset* 'he regularized'. Those are not numerous either, but words with ex-/w/ are not common anyway.

There is one class of verbs in which leveling with the input *b* does take place in stem-initial, postvocalic position, as in (10):

	(10)	Past 3rd Pers. Masc. Sing.	Fut. 3rd Pers. Masc. Sing.	Imperative Masc. Sing.	Gloss
		bilbel	*yevalbel*	*balbel*	'confuse'
or		*bilbel*	*yebalbel*	*balbel*	

bizbez	*yevazbez*	*bazbez*	'waste'
or *bizbez*	*yebazbez*	*bazbez*	

This only happens, however, in reduplicated verbs, where the first and second syllables of the stem are identical, except for the vowel, and leveling should be attributed to the tendency to keep reduplicated syllables identical (see Wilbur (1973) for support of this view). The same applies to stem-initial *k*, of course, but that is no surprise. Thus, we have:

(11)	Past 3rd Pers. Masc. Sing.	Fut. 3rd Pers. Masc. Sing.	Imperative Masc. Sing.	Gloss
	kilkel	*mexalkel*	*kalkel*	'support'
or	*kilkel*	*mekalkel*	*kalkel*	
	kiškeš	*mexaškeš*	*kaškeš*	'wag'
or	*kiškeš*	*mekaškeš*	*kaškeš*	

As expected from the nature of the relevant opacity, i.e. apparent overapplication, $p \sim f$ alternations are also subject to leveling with the output only, as we can see in (12):

(12)	Past 3rd Pers. Masc. Sing.	Fut. 3rd Pers. Masc. Sing.	Imperative Masc. Sing.	Gloss
	pitéax	*yefatéax*	*patéax*	'develop'
or	*fitéax*	*yefatéax*	*fatéax*	
but not	*pitéax*	**yepatéax*	*patéax*	
	perek	*yefarek*	*parek*	'pull apart'
or	*firek*	*yefarek*	*farek*	
but not	*perek*	**yeparek*	*parek*	
	pišet	*yefašet*	*pašet*	'simplify'
or	*fišet*	*yefašet*	*fašet*	
but not	*pišet*	**yepašet*	*pašet*	
	pister	*yefaster*	*paster*	'pasteurize'
or	*fister*	*yefaster*	*faster*	
but not	*pister*	**yepaster*	*paster*	
	patax	*yiftax*	*ptax*	'open'
or	*fatax*	*yiftax*	*ftax*	(child speech only)
but not	*patax*	**yiptax*	*ptax*	

Once again, leveling is very common in *pi^ʔel*, since this is where the opacity-causing borrowed verbs with initial *f* are realized. I know of no borrowed verb with initial *f* in *pa^ʔal*. If we add to that the reluctance to level with the unmarked *pa^ʔal* form, we can see why leveling with *f* in *pa^ʔal* is restricted to child speech, and in fact to a single verb, *patax*. ??*fatar* 'he solved' for *patar,* for instance (cf. *yiftor* 'he will solve'), or ??*fagaš* 'he met' for *pagaš* (cf. *yifgoš* 'he will meet'), are marginal even for children.

As is the case with *b ~ v*, leveling with the input may take place only in reduplicated verbs, to keep the reduplicated syllables identical, as in (13):

(13)	Past 3rd Pers. Masc. Sing.	Fut. 3rd Pers. Masc. Sing.	Gloss
	pitpet	*yefatpet*	'talk too much, chatter'
or	*pitpet*	*yepatpet*	
	pikpek	*yefakpek*	'doubt'
or	*pikpek*	*yepakpek*	

In non-automatic derivations in which one alternant has a spirant in stem-initial postvocalic position, analogy hardly ever applies. Thus, for instance, an alternation like *katav* 'he wrote' ~ *mixtav* 'letter' is never leveled, i.e. we never get **miktav* (*xatav,* as explained above, is possible, but certainly does not result from analogy with *mixtav*). The group of nouns realized in the canonical *mi*+CC*a*C pattern cannot be productively derived from parallel verbs in the *pa^ʔal* verb pattern—it is hardly predictable when such a relationship would in fact exist. Similarly, in pairs like *bóreg* 'screw' and *mavreg* 'screwdriver' or *patax* 'he opened' and *maftéax* 'key', *mavreg* and *maftéax* never become **mabreg* or **maptéax* respectively. Another example: in *katav* 'he wrote' ~ *taxtiv* 'dictate' (N), *balat* 'it projected' ~ *tavlit* 'relief (map)', *pakad* 'he ordered' ~ *tafkid* 'assignment, job', leveling into **taktiv, *tablit* or **tapkid* respectively is impossible. This is all regardless of how opaque spirantization is with regard to each of these forms.

There exist, however, automatic derivations involving spirantization in stem-initial postvocalic position which *are* subject to analogy. To go by the inflection-to-derivation continuum suggested above, the most obvious cases are those involving the infinitives of each of the conjugations concerned. The relationship between a finite form and its infinitive is on the border between inflection (in its narrow sense) and derivation, and is completely automatic. In addition, there is normally great formal resemblance between the infinitive and the future stem. We would expect infinitives, then, to be subject to the same type of leveling we have within the finite inflectional paradigm, as in (14):

(14)	Past 3rd Pers. Masc. Sing.	Fut. 3rd Pers. Masc. Sing.	Infinitive	Gloss
	katav	*yixtov*	*lixtov*	'write'
or	*katav*	*yiktov*	*liktov*	
	kiven	*yexaven*	*lexaven*	'aim'
or	*kiven*	*yekaven*	*lekaven*	

$b \sim v$ and $p \sim f$ are not similarly affected. The reason is, again, in their being transparent owing to the absence in *paʔal* as well as in *piʔel* of exceptions involving inapplication.

Another example of an automatic derivation of this type is the relationship between verbs of the *paʔal* conjugation and their nominalizations. Since this relationship is quite regular, we may have analogy as in (15). Word-initial x and f are restricted to child speech, though.

(15) *katav* 'he wrote'   *yixtov* 'he will write'   *ktiva* 'writing'
or   *katav*   *yiktov*   *ktiva*
or   *xatav*   *yixtov*   *xtiva*

     karat 'he cut off'   *yixrot* 'he will cut off'   *krita* 'cutting off'
or   *karat*   *yikrot*   *krita*
or   *??xarat*   *yixrot*   *xrita*

     kafaf/kofef 'he bent'   *yixpof/yexofef* 'he will bend'   *kfifa* 'bending'
or   *kafaf*   *yikpof/yikfof/yekofef*   *kfifa*
or   *??xafaf/??xofef*   *yixpof/yixfof/yexofef*   *xfifa*

     patax 'he opened'   *yiftax* 'he will open'   *ptixa* 'opening'
or   *fatax*   *yiftax*   *ftixa*

It was already mentioned that the reluctance to use *xarat* is due to avoidance of homonymity—*xarat* is a separate verb, meaning 'he engraved'. The marginality of *??xafaf/??xofef* can be explained similarly—*xafaf* with ex-/ħ/ means 'he shampooed'. As explained above, b is not leveled with v in *paʔal* since within *paʔal* very little opacity is involved. For the same reason, *patax* is the only *paʔal* verb to which leveling with f applies. In both cases, no leveling with a stop would be expected to apply, since there would be no apparent inapplication to cause it.

In the absence of a *paʔal* verb, the CC*i*C+*a* noun may analogize with a *piʔel* verb, as in (16).

(16) *kibes* 'he laundered'   *yexabes* 'he will launder'   *kvisa* 'laundry, laundering'
or   *kibes*   *yekabes*   *kvisa*
or   *xibes*   *yexabes*   *xvisa*

But normally, *piʔel* verbs have their own nominalization pattern, C*i*C*u*C, as in (17).

(17) *kibed* 'he respected'   *yexabed* 'he will respect'   *kibud* 'respect, respecting'
or   *kibed*   *yekabed*   *kibud*
or   *xibed*   *yexabed*   *xibud*

	kiven 'he aimed'	*yexaven* 'he will aim'	*kivun* 'aim, direction, directing'
or	*kiven*	*yekaven*	*kivun*
or	*xiven*	*yexaven*	*xivun*
	bikeš 'he asked'	*yevakeš* 'he will ask'	*bikuš* 'asking, demand'
or	*vikeš*	*yevakeš*	*vikuš*
	bitel 'he cancelled'	*yevatel* 'he will cancel'	*bitul* 'cancelling'
or	*vitel*	*yevatel*	*vitul*
	pitéax 'he developed'	*yefatéax* 'he will develop'	*pitúax* 'developing, development'
or	*fitéax*	*yefatéax*	*fitúax*
	perek 'he pulled apart'	*yefarek* 'he will pull apart'	*peruk* 'pulling apart'
or	*firek/ferek*	*yefarek*	*firuk/feruk*

An illustration of a somewhat less automatic inter-paradigmatic relationship is between *paʔal* and *nifʔal*. Pairs of *paʔal* and *nifʔal* forms, though belonging to different inflections, may be said to be subject to analogy, since it is often the case that the latter is the passive counterpart of the former, and this active-passive relationship is quite regular. Thus, for instance, we find sub-standard analogy as in (18), especially among children. (Once more, *b ~ v* and *p ~ f* are not affected, owing to the absence in *nifʔal* as well as in *paʔal* of exceptions involving inapplication.)

(18)	*katav* 'he wrote'	*nixtav* 'it was written'
or	*katav*	*niktav*
	karax 'he bound'	*nixrax* 'it was bound'
or	*karax*	*nikrax*
	kavaš 'he conquered'	*nixbas* 'it was conquered'
or	*kavaš*	*nikbaš/nikvaš*

However, what looks like *paʔal-nifʔal* analogy could also be explained by purely intra-paradigmatic factors such as the existence of *p* in the same position in the future of *nifʔal*, e.g. *nixtav ~ yikatev* 'it will be written'.

The *paʔal-hifʔil* relationship is even less automatic, and is thus less likely to be subject to analogy. *Hifʔil* is sufficiently productive for children to allow analogy with *paʔal, piʔel* or with related nouns, as in (19):

(19) *kaʔas* 'he was angry'~ *hixʔis* 'he annoyed' ~ *hikʔis*

     kiʔer 'he made ugly'~ *hixʔir* 'he made ugly' (marginal even for child speech) ~ *hikʔir*

     késef 'silver'~ *hixsif* 'he silver-coated' ~ *hiksif*

But such analogy is rare in adult speech, since relationships like *paʔal-hifʔil* have to be marked lexically. Thus, we never find adult alternations as in (20), not even in the most marginal sub-standard varieties.

(20) *katav* 'he wrote' ~ *hixtiv* 'he dictated' ~ **hiktiv*

      kašal 'he failed' (int.) ~ *hixšil* 'he failed' (tr.) ~ **hikšil*

2.3. Spirantization immediately following a word-initial consonant, and postvocalically in second radicals in *paʔal* and *nifʔal*

The position immediately following a word-initial consonant (where in Biblical Hebrew, there was an intervening schwa) is normally occupied by *x, v, f* rather than *k, b, p*. Most of the paradigms concerned, however, do not display stop-spirant alternation, since the alternants concerned contain spirants as well, e.g. *kavur* 'buried' (pres. masc. sing.) ~ *kvura* (pres. fem. sing.) ~ *kvurim* (pres. masc. pl.) ~ *kvurot* (pres. fem. pl.), and the question of leveling is irrelevant. There is one group of alternating forms—but as it is also the same group in which the second radical alternates in *paʔal* and *nifʔal*, and the forms concerned belong to the same respective paradigms, I will treat both cases together.

(21) Conj.	Past 3rd Pers. Masc. Sing.	Fut. 2nd Pers. Masc. Sing.	Imp. Masc. Sing.	Gloss
paʔal	*šaxav*	*tiškav*	*šxav*	'lie down'
	zaxar	*tizkor*	*zxor*	'remember' (stative)
	šaxax	*tiškax*	*šxax*	'forget'
	maxar	*timkor*	*mxor/mexor*	'sell'
	raxav	*tirkav*	*rexav*	'ride'
	laxad	*tilkod*	*lexod*	'catch'
	xaxar	*taxkor*	*xaxor*	'lease'
	xaxax	*taxkox*	*xaxox*	'deliberate'
	šavar	*tišbor*	*švor*	'break'
	saval	*tisbol*	*svol*	'suffer'
	kavar	*tikbor*	*kvor*	'bury'
	gavar	*tigbor*	*gvor*	'overcome'
	cavar	*ticbor*	*cvor*	'accumulate'
	šavat	*tišbot*	*švot*	'strike'
	lavaš	*tilbaš*	*levaš*	'wear'
	naval	*tinbol*	*nvol/nevol*	'wither'
	šafax	*tišpox*	*šfox*	'spill'
	safar	*tispor*	*sfor*	'count'
	dafak	*tidpok*	*dfok*	'knock'
	kafac	*tikpoc*	*kfoc*	'jump'

	tafas	titpos	tfos	'catch'
	šafat	*tišpot*	*šfot*	'judge'
	safag	*tispog*	*sfog*	'absorb'
	tafar	*titpor*	*tfor*	'sew'
	kafar	*tixpor*	*kfor*	'deny'
	cafar	*ticpor*	*cfor*	'honk'
nif'al	*niškav*	*tišaxev*	*hišaxev*	'lie down'
	nizkar	*tizaxer*	*hizaxer*	'recall, suddenly remember'
	niškax	*tišaxax*	*hišaxax*	'be forgotten'
	nimkar	*timaxer*	*himaxer*	'be sold'
	nilkad	*tilaxed*	*hilaxed*	'be caught'
	nexkar	*texaxer*	*(hexaxer)*	'be leased'
	nišbar	*tišaver*	*hišaver*	'be broken'
	nisbal	*tisavel*	*(hisavel)*	'be suffered'
	nikbar	*tikaver*	*hikaver*	'be buried'
	nicbar	*ticaver*	*(hicaver)*	'be accumulated'
	nilbaš	*tilaveš*	*(hilaveš)*	'be worn'
	nišpax	*tišafex*	*hišafex*	'be spilled'
	nispar	*tisafer*	*(hisafer)*	'be counted'
	nidpak	*tidafek*	*(hidafek)*	'be knocked, fucked'
	nitpas	*titafes*	*hitafes*	'be caught'
	nispag	*tisafeg*	*hisafeg*	'be absorbed'
	nišpat	*tišafet*	*hišafet*	'be judged'
	nitpar	*titafer*	*(hitafer)*	'be sewn'

The three columns are not related to each other with equal strength. Immediate formal and functional relationship exists, as expected, between the future and imperative on the one hand and to a lesser extent between past and future forms on the other. The formal and functional relationship between past and imperative forms seems to be the least direct one.

Leveling with the output may apply throughout, since all that is involved is replacing the stop by a spirant in the future form, and since the past form is the unmarked base in the past-future relationship, such leveling is expected. It may also be argued that the imperative spirant reinforces this tendency, and that at the same time, the future is leveled with the unmarked imperative. I doubt whether this is the case, however, for the following reasons. First, because the unleveled form of the imperative in stem-initial position (2.2.) contains *k, b, p,* and still the future is *not* leveled with the imperative in the case of *b* and *p* (i.e. no **yibdok, *yiptax*). Second, many of the imperative forms are hardly used; it is the future form that is heard instead, and it is not very likely that the direction of leveling would be determined by the less frequent forms.

Each of the three stops may be leveled with the corresponding spirant, then. We hear *tirxav, timxor, tilxod,*
tišxav, tizxor, as well as *tišvor, tisvol, tikvor, tigvor, ticvor, tišvot, tilvaš, tinvol*—and *tišfox, tišfor, tidfok, tikfoc,*
titfos, tišfot, tisfog, titfor, tikfor, ticfor. This is expected not only because it implies leveling with the unmarked
form, but also because apparent overapplication causes opacity in each case: ex-/ħ/ occurs in forms like *tivxon/tivxan*
'you will examine', *timxok/timxak* 'you will erase', etc., ex-/w/ in *tilve* 'you will borrow', *tigva* 'you will die', and
f in borrowed and colloquial verbs such as *tilfen* 'he telephoned', *fisfes* 'he missed'. In stem-initial position (2.2.),
all three stops are subject to leveling with spirants as well owing to similar opacity, but these opacity considerations
overrule leveling with the unmarked past forms. Perhaps this is some indication, then, that opacity might outweigh
the tendency to level with the unmarked form when the two are in conflict, but since this is not total leveling, but
rather leveling of one segment only, it hardly constitutes ample evidence.

There is also the question of why there is a considerable difference in acceptability between words with leveled *k,*
b and *p,* with acceptability increasing in this same order: *timxor, tilxod,* etc. are more marginal than *tišvor, tisvol,*
etc., and the latter are not as widely used as *tišfox, tisfor,* etc. In fact, in some forms involving *p~f,* the leveled forms
with *f* have actually replaced the corresponding unleveled forms in normal usage: *tidfok, tikfoc, titfos, titfor.* These
acceptability differences are even sharper in *nifʔal: nišxav, nizxar,* etc. are quite marginal, *nišvar, nisval,* etc. are more
acceptable, and *nišfax, nisfar* even better. *nidfak, nitfas* and *nitfar* actually replace their unleveled counterparts.
Barkai (1978) attributes this to a tendency for avoidance of semantic opacity, which diminishes from *k* to *p:*
as a second radical, *x* would be potentially ambiguous between *x* from *k* and *x* from ex-/ħ/. So would *v* from *b,*
but only to some extent, since *v* is rarely realized as second radical in *paʔal* or *nifʔal,* and verbs with ex-/w/ are not
so common anyway. In the case of *f* from *p,* no ambiguity would ever arise, and thus there is no semantic reason
for curbing leveling with *f.* But as indicated before, avoidance of homonymity is only a tendency, and although it may
very well explain *some* phenomena, it might also arbitrarily ignore other cases to which it should have been equally
applicable. In the absence of a better explanation, however, I will assume that Barkai's explanation is correct and
that reasons for the principle of avoidance of homonymity not operating where it should could indeed be found.

Leveling with *k, b, p* is less common than leveling with the corresponding spirants. In the case of the imperative,
there seem to be two conflicting tendencies: on the one hand, the occurrence of a spirant after a *consonant* makes
the *original* spirantization rule opaque; on the other hand, the strong tendency in native words for the second
segment in an initial CC cluster to be a spirant rather than the corresponding stop may be interpreted as a
reformulated sub-rule of spirantization of considerable productivity, and in the imperative such a rule would be
transparent. There is also the possible leveling with the *future* as a base form. As a result, spirants in some forms
may be leveled with stops, other may not: we hear *škav, zkor, škax, šbor, sbol, špox, spor.* All other levelings of
this type are either marginal, e.g. *kbor, gbor, cbor, šbot, kpoc, špot, spog,* or impossible, e.g. **lebaš, *nebol, *dpok,*
??kpor. The situation is not different in the future and imperative of *nifʔal: tišakax, tilaked, texaker, tišaber, tišapex,*
and *tisaper* are acceptable, all other levelings with stops are not.

In the past, leveling with stops in even less frequent. Only the following are heard: *lakad, xakar, xakax, šabar*
ʔlabaš, šapax, sapar. xakar and *xakax* may be attributed to an extension of the *x-x* dissimilation rule operating
in /mixxol/ > *mikxol* 'painting brush', /hixxiš/ > *hikxiš* 'he denied', etc., and the rest, except for *lakad,* are more
typical of child speech than of adult leveling. This again seems to support the feeling most adults still have, that
past, third person singular masculine *paʔal* forms are basic.

In non-automatic derivations, no analogy occurs. In *zaxar* 'he remembered'~*mazkir* 'secretary', *šavar* 'he broke'
~*mašber* 'crisis', *šafax* 'he spilled'~*mašpex* 'watering can', we never get **mazxir, *mašver* or **mašfex* respectively.
Similarly, in *zaxar* 'he remembered'~*tizkóret* 'reminder', *lavaš* 'he wore'~*tilbóšet* 'clothes', *šafax* 'he spilled'~

tišpóxet 'semen' (colloq.), there are no variants such as ***tizxóret*, **tilvóšet* or ***tišfóxet* respectively. But there are automatic derivations in which analogy may apply, though not commonly. We have nominalization as in (22):

(22)	Fut. 2nd Pers. Masc. Sing.	Related Gerund	Alternative Pronunciation	Gloss
	tiškav	*xiva*	*škiva*	'lie down'
	tizkor	*zxira*	*zkira*	'remember'
	tiškax	*xixa*	*škixa*	'forget'
	tilkod	*lexida*	*lekida*	'catch'
	tišbor	*švira*	*šbira*	'break'

Only *škiva*, however, is reasonably well established; the rest are rather marginal. I believe that the scarcity of analogy here is due to the fact that nominalizations normally follow the unmarked past form, and that since the latter is rarely leveled with a stop, related nominalizations do not often undergo leveling with stops either.

Another automatic derivation is of adjectives and participles related to *paʔal*. Here and there such derivational alternations may be analogized, as in (23):

(23)	Past 3rd Pers. Masc. Sing.	Alternative Pronunciation	Fut. 3rd Pers. Masc. Sing.	Passive Participle/ Adj. Masc. Sing.	Alternative Pronunciation	Gloss
	laxad	*lakad*	*yilkod*	*laxud*	*lakud*	'catch'
	xaxar	*xakar*	*yaxkor*	*xaxur*	*xakur*	'lease'
	šavar	*šabar*	*yišbor*	*šavur*	*šabur*	'break'
	šafax	*šapax*	*yišpox*	*šafux*	*šapux*	'spill'
	safar	*sapar*	*yispor*	*safur*	*sapur*	'count'

Analogy of related adjectives and participles applies more or less in those cases (introduced above) in which the unmarked past form may be leveled with a stop.

Again, as the relationship between finite forms and their infinitives is as automatic as any inflectional relationship, it is often subject to leveling, almost to the same extent as intra-paradigmatic alternations are:

(24)	Past 3rd Pers. Masc. Sing.	Fut. 2nd Pers. Masc. Sing.	Infinitive	Gloss
	maxar	*timkor*	*limkor*	'sell'
or	*maxar*	*timxor*	*limxor*	
	cavar	*ticbor*	*licbor*	'accumulate'
or	*cavar*	*ticvor*	*licvor*	
	šafat	*tišpot*	*lišpot*	'judge'
or	*šafat*	*tišfot*	*lišfot*	

3. *n*-DELETION

n-deletion applies stem-initially before another consonant.

Within inflections, alternations are found in *paʔal* and *nifʔal*, as can be seen in (25).

(25) Conj.	Past 3rd Pers. Masc. Sing.	Fut. 3rd Pers. Masc. Sing.	Imp. Masc. Sing.	Infin.	Gloss
paʔal	nafal	yipol	n(e)fol/pol	lipol	'fall'
	nasa	yisa	n(e)sa/sa	linsóa/lisóa	'go, ride (car)'
	nasa	yisa	n(e)sa/sa	laset	'carry'
	naga	yiga	n(e)ga/ga	lingóa/ligóa/lagáat	'touch'
	nigaš	yigaš	gaš	lagéšet	'approach'
	nacar	yicor	n(e)cor/cor	lincor/licor	'guard, save'
	natan	yiten	ten	latet	'give'
	našax	yišox	n(e)šox	linšox	'bite'
	nakam	yikom	n(e)kom	linkom	'revenge'
	našar	yišor	n(e)šor	linšor	'fall off'
	nazal	yizol	n(e)zol	linzol/lizol	'leak'
	natal	yitol	n(e)tol/tol	lintol/litol	'take, wash'
	našak	yišak	šak	linšok	'kiss'
nifʔal	nical	yinacel	hinacel	lehinacel	'be saved'
	nitan	yinaten	hinaten	lehinaten	'be given'
	nikam	yinakem	hinakem	lehinakem	'be revenged'
	nišax	yinašex	hinašex	lehinašex	'be bitten'

In Biblical Hebrew, *n*-deletion applied fairly regularly to stem-initial *n* followed by a non-low consonant, i.e. not to *yinḥal* 'he will inherit', *yinhag* 'he will treat, behave', *yinʕal* 'he will lock', *yinʔaf* 'he will commit adultery', etc., except for imperatives and infinitives containing the stem-vowel *o*. There were sporadic exceptions here and there, particularly in non-colloquial pausal forms. In Modern Hebrew, however, it seems to have become quite minor, and thus quite opaque, as soon as the language was revived. Exceptions to it, as in (26),

(26)	Past 3rd Pers. Masc. Sing.	Fur. 3rd Pers. Masc. Sing.	Gloss
	nagas	yingos	'nibble, have a bite'
	navat	yinvot	'bud'
	navax	yinbax/yinvax	'bark'
	našam	yinšom	'breathe'

clearly outnumber the cases which undergo *n*-deletion (see Barkai (1975) for further illustrations and discussion). *n* would be preserved in the future of new verbs with stem-initial *n*, but since *paʔal* is not very productive today, there are few recent verbs of this kind. Leveling with the input of older forms, however, is very extensive. Thus, *yicor, yišox, yikom* and *yišor* above are *always* replaced by *yincor, yinšox, yinkom* and *yinšor* respectively in colloquial speech, and *yizol, yitol* and *yisa* ('carry') are in free variation with *yinzol, yintol* and *yinsa* respectively. Furthermore, *yisa* ('ride') and *yinsa* are variants in sub-standard speech, and children have either *yiga* or *yinga,* and sometimes even *yinpol* as a variant of *yipol.* Similarly, *nifʔal* past forms have variants like *ninkam* and *ninšax* for *nikam* and *nišax* respectively. Everything indicates that the direction of leveling should be with the input: the input is the unmarked base form, and since *n*-deletion is rendered opaque by inapplication of spirantization to imperatives and infinitives with the stem-vowel *o,* which is certainly not phonetically conditioned, and by many forms to which *n*-deletion was supposed to apply in Modern Hebrew but never did, we would again predict leveling with the input. Inapplication would probably be expected whenever minor rules are involved, since it implies analogy with the majority of cases. In our case, another factor intervenes: deletion of the initial *n* in forms like *nasa* 'he rode', or 'he carried', would cause reinterpretation as /ʔasa/ 'he made', since a word-initial vowel is always preceded by an underlying /ʔ/. Alternatively, if it were claimed that the whole first syllable should be lost in the past when leveling with the future takes place, the result would again be semantically ambiguous, since verbs with initial *n* might be interpreted as "hollow" verbs with the second radical lenited. Note that although the same might be said of the reduced imperative of some *n*-initial verbs (*sa, ga, cor,* etc.), the case of the imperative is different, since "hollow" verb imperatives have either *u* or *i,* which are never found in any reduced imperative of *n*-initial verbs.

Forms like *cor, pol* bring us to another development in *n*-deletion. As stated above, in Biblical Hebrew, *n*-deletion did not apply to imperatives and infinitives containing the stem-vowel *o,* i.e. beside imperatives like *sa, ga, gaš, šaq,* etc. and infinitives like *lagáʕat, lagéšet,* etc., there existed imperatives such as *nəfol, nəšor, nəqom,* etc., and infinitives such as *linpol, linšor, linqom,* respectively. As we can see from the second and third columns in (25) above, in Modern Hebrew some of these imperatives and infinitives are analogized with their respective future forms— at least in one case obligatorily (*lipol*), but normally optionally: *n(e)fol ~ pol, n(e)cor ~ cor, lincor ~ licor, linzol ~ lizol, n(e)tol ~ tol, lintol ~ litol,* etc. These are, of course, cases of leveling with the output. Such leveling is considerably rarer than leveling with the input since, as has already been pointed out, there are strong reasons for leveling involving the loss of *n*-deletion. Since the formal and functional relationship between the future and both imperatives and infinitives is stronger than the relationship between the past and the latter two, such leveling is not surprising, and it is also clear why it never extends to past forms.

Again, no analogy is attested in non-automatic derivations, e.g. in *naga* 'he touched' ~ *maga* 'touch', *nasa* 'he traveled/ carried' ~ *masa* 'trip/load', we never get **manga* or **mansa.* As in the case of stem-initial spirantization, the relationship between *paʔal* and *hifʔil* is somewhat productive for children, e.g. marginal *hinsia* for *hisia,* but not productive enough to allow analogy in adult speech, and thus in *nafal* 'he fell' ~ *hipil* 'he caused to fall', *naga* 'he touched' ~ *higía* 'he arrived', one does not find variants such as **hinpil* or **hingía.*

The more automatic active-passive inter-paradigmatic relationship of *paʔal-nifʔal* may be said to undergo analogy in adult speech, as in (27):

(27)	Unmarked *paʔal* Form	Unmarked *nifʔal* Form	Alternative Pronunciation	Gloss
	nakam	*nikam*	*ninkam*	'revenge/be revenged'
	našax	*nišax*	*ninšax*	'bite/be bitten'

But as can be seen above, it is at least equally probable that this leveling is with the *n* of the future and imperative of *nifʔal* itself.

4. LOWERING AND COPY IN THE ENVIRONMENT OF *x* FROM /ħ/

In Biblical Hebrew, the 'gutturals', i.e. the [+low] consonants, favored non-high vowels and/or breaking of sequences of [+low] consonants followed by consonants. I will not deal with the merger of /ʕ/ with /ʔ/ and with the synchronic loss of /ʔ/ anywhere except (optionally) before stressed vowels, which are too complex to handle here; I will restrict my discussion to synchronic lowering and copy in the environment of *x* from historical /ħ/.

In formal style, a prefix vowel before stem-initial *x* from /ħ/ is lowered and copied across that *x*, as in (28):

(28)	Conj.	3rd Pers. Masc. Sing.	Gloss
	paʔal	*yi+xzor > yaxazor*	'will return'
		yi+xšov > yaxašov	'will think'
	nifʔal	*ni+xšav > nexešav*	'was thought (of as)'
		ni+xlak > nexelak	'was divided'
	hifʔil	*hi+xzik > hexezik*	'held'
		hi+xlit > hexelit	'decided'

Abstract representations like /yi+xzor/, /ni+xšav/ or hi+xzik/ should be allowed in each of the three inflections, since *ya ~ yi, ne ~ ni* and *he ~ hi* in *paʔal, nifʔal* and *hifʔil* respectively when forms as in (28) "alternate" with corresponding regular forms realized in the respective paradigms: *yi+sgor, ni+sgar, hi+sgir*, etc. (people seem to be aware of relations between irregular and regular forms in verbal paradigms more than of similar relations in nominal canonical patterns). The opacity of lowering and copy is due to two factors. One is the /ħ/-*x* merger, which increases the number of exceptions due to inapplication, e.g. *yixtov, nixtav, hixtiv*, which result from spirantization of /k/. The second is the fact that there seem to be two degrees of lowering, one from *i* to *e* and one from *i* to *a*, depending on the particular paradigm, though generally lowering to a [+low] vowel in the environment of [+low] consonants is the more expected process (and indeed the one we still normally find elsewhere in formerly "guttural" environments). The *i > e* part is more opaque than the *i > a* one in the sense that it cannot be predicted which paradigms would be subject to it rather than to the more general "full" lowering. This is why *yaxazor* or *yaxašov* are never realized as **yixzor* or **yixšov* respectively, whereas the *hifʔil i* often surfaces today—*hexezik* and *hixzik* are variants and so are *hexelit* and *hixlit*. Since the opacity involved stems from what looks like inapplication, *hixzik* and *hixlit* could be considered leveling with the input, but obviously what in fact happens is leveling with *regular hifʔil* forms like *hi+sgir*.

Note, however, that the *nifʔal* cases, though not as resistant to loss as the *paʔal* cases, normally do not allow *i* to surface, e.g. *nexešav* and *nexelak* hardly ever become ?*nixšav* or ?*nixlak*. In a sense, then, the *hifʔil* cases are more opaque than both the *paʔal* and the *nifʔal* cases. It was proposed to me by Malachi Barkai (personal communication) that it may be explained by the absence or presence of *k ~ x* alternation in the respective paradigms: that because the velar in stem-initial position in *hifʔil* is *always x*, there is more reason for opacity of *x* from historical /ħ/, due to apparent inapplication, whereas in *paʔal* and *nifʔal k* alternates with *x*, and speakers know that those *x*'s that do not alternate with *k* are the ones that originated from /ħ/ and are thus less confused.

As far as copy is concerned, the forms *yaxazor, nexešav, hexezik,* etc. above are quite formal and are hardly found in colloquial Hebrew, which normally has *yaxzor, nexšav,* and *hexzik/hixzik* respectively. Only *hixzik,* however, involves actual leveling with regular forms—*hexzik, yaxzor,* and *nexšav* result from loss of copy, but as lowering is not lost as well, they can hardly be attributed to leveling with actual regular forms.

As explained above, leveling here is different from previous cases discussed above, since it is leveling with corresponding regular verb forms realized in the same verbal paradigm. In non-verbal forms, what is involved is juxtaposition with regular forms realized in the same canonical pattern. The implication of this for the claim that leveling depends on productivity is, presumably, that the less productive the canonical pattern, the less likely the leveling with regular forms realized in it.

In canonical forms of restricted productivity, lowering is hardly ever lost; copy is not lost either, except that there were cases to which copy was never applied to start with when the language was revived. Thus, *maxnak* 'stifling air' never started as ?*maxanak, taxkir* 'questioning' was never ?*taxakir,* and so on. But if we take words like *maxaze* 'play' and *maxane* 'camp', which underlyingly belong to the same canonical form as *mivne* 'building, structure' and *mifne* 'turn', we see that they are never realized as*maxze or *maxne respectively (except in the misguided hyper-correct use of the construct state) and certainly not as *mixze or *mixne. When only copy is involved, i.e. when the original vowel was *a* to start with, copy will not be lost either: *taxazit* 'forecast', which belongs to the same pattern as *tafnit* 'turn', may only vary with *taxzit* in the hypercorrect use of the construct state.

There are no non-verbal canonical patterns of considerable productivity in which lowering and copy would be relevant. In the *ha*+CCaC+*a* nominalization pattern of *hifʔil,* for instance (e.g. *haxlata* 'decision, deciding'), not even lowering has applied, since we are dealing with a basic *a,* and copy has never taken place either, not even in Biblical Hebrew.

5. VERB STRESS, AND VOWEL REDUCTION IN *paʔal*

In the Hebrew verb, when the suffix is +C# or +CV#, stress falls on the stem-final vowel: *katáv+ti* 'I wrote', *katáv+ta* 'you masc. sing. wrote', *katáv+nu* 'we wrote', *kaní+t* 'you fem. sing. bought', *nišbár+ti* 'I broke', *dibár+t* 'you fem. sing. spoke', *sudár+nu* 'we were arranged', *hisbár+ta* 'you masc. sing. explained', *hušpál+nu* 'we were humiliated', and so on.

In formal Hebrew, if the suffix not only begins with a consonant but also *ends* with one, i.e. when the suffix is +*tem* 'you plural' (very formally +*ten* for 'you fem. pl.'), it does not trigger stress assignment to the preceding vowel but rather attracts stress itself, e.g. *ktav+tém* 'you pl. wrote', *nišbar+tém* 'you pl. broke (int.)', *dibar+tém* 'you pl. spoke', and so on. In the case of *paʔal,* e.g. *ktav+tém* above, the vowel preceding the stem-vowel is deleted by an extension of the *a*-deletion rule for nouns and adjectives, which deletes *a* in an open syllable two syllables before a stressed suffix: /davar+ím/ 'things' (cf. *davar* 'thing') > *dvarím,* /katan+á/ 'small, fem. sing.' (cf. *katan* 'small, masc. sing.') > *ktaná,* etc. Alternatively, it is also possible that speakers could never see the inter-paradigm connection between *a*-deletion in nouns and adjectives and /katav+tém/ > *ktavtém,* and that the latter was conceived of as a very minor, irregular phenomenon right from the start.

In colloquial Hebrew, however, with CaCaC being the unmarked base form for *pa'al*, and indisputably so in the past of *pa'al*, leveling of forms like *ktavtém* with the rest of the past paradigm was unavoidable. The fact that *+ti*, *+ta* and *+t*, which are appended to CaCaC, show partial similarity to *+tem*, and that the latter two refer to second person as well, must have also helped. Leveling applies, then, in the direction of the unmarked form, and *a*-deletion is no longer extended to verbs. Since the unmarked form has stress assigned to the final vowel of the stem, wherever that vowel is preserved, **katav+tém* is quite opaque, and the *+tem* sub-part of the stress rule is lost in favor of the more general assignment to the stem-final vowel, i.e. *katávtem*, to correspond with *katávti*, *katávta*, *katávt*, etc.

6. SEGOLATE PLURAL

Segolate nouns are stressed penultimately when in isolation and normally end with an unstressed syllable containing *e*. Plural forms do not preserve that *e*, as can be seen in (29).

(29)	**Masc. Sing.**	**Masc. Pl.**	**Gloss**
	mélex	*mlaxim*	'king'
	kélev	*klavim*	'dog'
	kéves	*kvasim*	'sheep' (masc.)
	yéled	*yeladim*	'boy'
	Fem. Sing.	**Fem. Pl.**	**Gloss**
	malka	*mlaxot*	'queen'
	kalba	*klavot*	'bitch'
	kivsa	*kvasot*	'ewe'
	yalda	*yeladot*	'girl'
	šixva	*šxavot*	'layer'
	simla	*smalot*	'dress'

To form the plural of both masculine and feminine forms, one introduces *a* in between the second and third consonant and deletes the initial vowel—two simultaneous or consecutive rules restricted to the segolate class (unless one incorporates the second with the *a*-deletion rule mentioned above).

Although segolate plural formation is highly morphologized in Modern Hebrew, and can hardly be motivated phonetically, there is little reason for opacity in masculine segolates. Indeed one finds plurals of non-segolates which look as if they were masculine segolates, e.g. *davar* 'thing'~ *dvarim* 'things', *katan* 'small'~ *ktanim* 'small, pl.', but pairs like *davar~dvarim* form a large, distinctive group, and their singular forms can never be confused with segolate singulars (there would at least be a stress difference). On the other hand, one finds many non-segolate forms whose singular cannot be distinguished from singular *feminine* segolates but which do not undergo segolate plural formation: *kasda* 'helmet'~ *kasdot* 'helmets', *tikva* 'hope'~ *tikvot* 'hopes', *kumta* 'cap'~ *kumtot* 'caps', etc. It is quite hard for speakers to distinguish between these and feminine segolates, and since *kasdot*, etc. look like cases of inapplication of segolate plural formation, plurals of feminine segolates are often leveled with the unmarked singular input, so that *malkot* and *kalbot* actually replace *mlaxot* and *klavot* respectively, and *kivsot* and *šixvot* vary with *kvasot* and *šxavot* respectively. Not all plural forms of feminine segolates undergo leveling: *yaldot* and *simlot* can only be found in the rarely used construct-state form. Still, the plural forms of many feminine segolates *are* leveled with the singular, and the tendency seems to be on the increase. Since this singular-plural relationship is paradigmatic, and thus automatic, leveling would indeed be expected in the presence of the opacity caused by plural forms of the *kasdot* type.

7. ANALOGY IN WORD-FORMATION

There seems to exist a class of exceptions to the claim that the extent of analogical change depends on the capability to automatically derive alternating forms from each other. There is quite a number of denominative verbs (and a few nouns derived from other nouns) which undergo analogy with their underlying nouns although formation of denominative verbs is not that automatic (it is somewhat productive, as shown in Bolozky (1978), but certainly not to the degree of automaticity). Thus, in *pi?el* and *hitpa?el*, where spirantization is always blocked in the second radical, it does apply in denominative verbs in analogy with the source noun:

(30) *roxel* 'pedlar'   > *rixel* 'he gossipped'   not *rikel

      šavac 'heart attack'   > *hištavec* 'he had a heart attack' not *hištabec (acceptable only when
                                                                      derived from *šibec* 'he placed, assigned')

      xaver 'friend'   > *hitxaver* 'he befriended'   not *hitxaber (acceptable only when
                                                                      derived from *xiber* 'he joined')

and in

(31) *koxav* 'star'   > *kixev* 'he starred'   not *kikev
                               > *mekaxev* 'he stars'   not *mexakev

spirantization not only applies where it should not, but also does not apply stem-initially, where it *should* have applied.

There is also an obvious case of an abstract noun derived from another noun:

(32) *néfeš* 'soul'   > *hanfašā* 'animation'   not *hanpaša

Such cases, however, do not really constitute counterexamples to the automaticity claim. They all involve word-formation, and are different from the analogies dealt with above in at least one important respect: there are no corresponding alternative forms that have *not* undergone analogy, i.e. analogy has always been obligatory for them. This suggests that word-formation analogy will probably have to be treated separately, and consequently may not necessarily be subject to the same constraints as regular "optional" analogy. If word-formation analogy is treated separately, the correlation between analogy and productivity *in word-formation* can still be maintained: analogical word-formation is most common in *pi?el*, since *pi?el* is the most productive conjugation today (cf. Bolozky (1978)).

8. CONCLUSION

To conclude, ongoing changes in Modern Hebrew support the principle of paradigm coherence and indicate that to a large extent leveling is a function of both the automaticity of the relationships concerned and of the relevant opacity. It has also been shown that if the leveling direction cannot be explained by reference to the unmarked base form, it can often be attributed to the nature of opacity involved. What would be interesting for future research is to find out the extent to which leveling and its direction can be predicted by similar considerations in other languages and perhaps try to establish some hierarchical order among the factors involved.

REFERENCES

Barkai, M. 1975. "On phonological representations, rules and opacity." *Lingua* 37:363-376.

Barkai, M. 1978. "Phonological opacity vs. semantic transparency: two cases from Israeli Hebrew." *Lingua* 44:363-378.

Ben-Horin, G. and S. Bolozky. 1972. "Hebrew *b, p, k*—rule opacity or data opacity?" *Hebrew Computational Linguistics* 5:24-35.

Blau, Y. 1972. *Torat Hahege Vehatsurot.* Hakibbuts Hameuchad.

Bolozky, S. 1977. "Fast speech as a function of tempo in natural generative phonology." *Journal of Linguistics* 13:217-238.

Bolozky, S. 1978. "Word-formation strategies in the Hebrew verb system: denominative verbs." *Afroasiatic Linguistics* 5(3):111-136.

de Chene, B. 1975. "The treatment of analogy in a formal grammar." *Papers from the 11th meeting of the Chicago Linguistic Society,* pp. 152-164. Chicago: Univeristy of Chicago Linguistic Society.

Harris, J. "On the order of certain phonological rules in Spanish." In S. Anderson and P. Kiparsky (eds.), *A Festschrift for Morris Halle,* pp. 59-76. New York: Holt.

Hooper, J. 1976. *An Introduction to Natural Generative Phonology.* New York: Academic Press.

Kautzsch, E. 1909. *Gesenius' Hebrew Grammar.* Translated by A. E. Cowley. London: Oxford University Press.

King, R. 1969. *Historical Linguistics and Generative Grammar.* Englewood Cliffs, New Jersey: Prentice Hall.

King, R. 1972. "A note on opacity and paradigm regularity." *Linguistic Inquiry* 3:535-539.

Kiparsky, P. 1971. "Historical linguistics." In W. O. Dingwall (ed.), *A Survey of Linguistic Science,* pp. 577-649. University of Maryland Press.

Kiparsky, P. 1972. "Explanation in phonology." In S. Peters (ed.), *Goals of Linguistic Theory,* pp. 189-227. Englewood Cliffs, New Jersey: Prentice Hall.

Kiparsky, P. 1973. "Phonological representations." In O. Fujimura (ed.), *Three Dimensions of Linguistic Theory,* pp. 1-136. Tokyo: TEC Company.

Kiparsky, P. 1974. "On the evaluation measure." *Papers from the Parasession on Natural Phonology of the Chicago Linguistic Society,* pp. 328-337. Chicago: University of Chicago Linguistic Society.

Miller, G. 1973. "On the motivation of phonological change." In B. Kachru et al. (eds.), *Issues in Linguistics: Papers in Honor of Henry and Renee Kahane,* pp. 686-718. Urbana, Illinois: University of Illinois Press.

Skousen, R. 1975. *Substantive Evidence in Phonology.* The Hague: Mouton.

Vennemann, T. 1972a. "Phonetic analogy and conceptual analogy." In T. Vennemann and T. Wilbur (eds.), *Schuchardt, the Neogrammarians and the Transformational Theory of Phonological Change,* pp. 181-204. Frankfurt: Athenaeum.

Vennemann, T. 1972b. "Rule inversion." *Lingua* 29:209-242.

Vennemann, T. 1974a. "Phonological concreteness in natural generative grammar." In R. Shuy and C. J. Bailey (eds.), *Toward Tomorrow's Linguistics,* pp. 202-219. Washington, D.C.: Georgetown University Press.

Vennemann, T. 1974b. "Restructuring." *Lingua* 33:137-156.

Wanner, D. 1972. "The derivation of inflectional paradigms in Italian." In J. Casagrande and B. Saciuk (eds.), *Generative Studies in Romance Languages,* pp. 293-318. Newbury House.

Wilbur, R. 1973. "The phonology of reduplication." Bloomingtom: Indiana University Linguistics Club.

ORIENTAL ISRAELI HEBREW:
A Study in Phonetics[1]

by
Monica S. Devens
Pomona College

Native Israeli Hebrew has been described as existing in two varieties: General Israeli Hebrew (GIH) and Oriental Israeli Hebrew (OIH). OIH has classically been defined as the variety spoken by many Israelis of Middle Eastern and North African backgrounds. Its principal phonetic features were said to be: maintenance of the classical Hebrew pharyngeals (/ħ/ and /ʕ/) and a dental articulation of /r/.

This description is no longer valid. While maintenance of /ħ/ is the single, most outstanding mark of OIH, /ʕ/ has been drastically curtailed. The phonetic realizations of /ʕ/ must also be re-examined. A dental articulation of /r/ no longer sets OIH apart from GIH. Finally, differences in intonation—both in pattern and in frequency of pattern—are very significant.

CONTENTS

1. INTRODUCTION

Blanc (1964) divided native Israeli Hebrew into two broad categories: "General Israeli" and "Oriental Israeli."[2] General Israeli Hebrew (henceforth, GIH) was so called because, while it was originally the variety spoken by people of European stock, it had spread to the extent that speakers could no longer be identified as to geographic origin. Oriental Israeli Hebrew (henceforth, OIH), on the other hand, was found only among people of Middle Eastern and North African backgrounds, and while further differentiation within these various Oriental populations was unknown, it had not been excluded.

While no case of genuine acquisition of OIH by a speaker of non-Oriental background was known to Blanc, it was not unusual to hear certain phones of OIH intermittently in the speech of educated non-Oriental individuals, especially those professionally involved with the Hebrew language. This was due to the fact that the phonemic system of OIH was considered more "authentic" and its adoption was being strongly advocated in language and government circles. At the time, this advocacy had failed to achieve any widespread results and movement between the two varieties was strictly one-way, i.e. towards GIH.

Differences between the two varieties were said to exist in many areas of speech (phonetics, phonology, grammar and lexicon). Only phonetics and phonology will be treated in this paper. According to Blanc, OIH possessed two additional phonemes, /ħ/ and /ʕ/. In GIH, /ħ/ had shifted to the velar position, becoming /x/. /ʕ/ had merged with /ʔ/, both realized as [ʔ] or, more commonly, zero. Blanc did note that some OIH speakers maintained /ʕ/ only inconsistently. Furthermore, /r/ was realized, as a rule, as [ɾ] in OIH and [ʁ] in GIH. Some of the latter also showed [ɾ], however.

Blanc's 1964 piece was not the first in which Israeli Hebrew was described in this way. Both Blanc himself (1957b) and Morag (1959) had already presented more or less the same view. But the 1964 contribution was of great significance because it was the first publication of actual data (in the form of well-annotated texts) supporting the description.

In the fifteen years that have passed since Blanc's article, relatively little has been published on the phonetics of Israeli Hebrew. The work that has appeared, while for the most part acknowledging the existence of two varieties, has dealt exclusively with GIH, under one name or another.[3] OIH continues to be described, in passing, as it was in 1964 (Blanc 1973, Morag 1972-73, Téné 1968). This paper presents the results of a much broader re-examination of OIH.

2. METHODOLOGY

Ten native speakers of Hebrew (second and third generation Israelis) were studied. Seven were OIH speakers and three were GIH speakers. Since the question of uniformity within OIH was to be examined, a wide range of national backgrounds was sought. The composition of the OIH sample was as follows: one person of Moroccan extraction, two people of Yemenite extraction, one person of Iraqi extraction, one person of Kurdish/Iraqi extraction, and two people of mixed Middle Eastern backgrounds. The GIH group included two people of Iraqi extraction and one person of Polish extraction. Both OIH and GIH speakers were studied because it was felt that the published accounts were not extensive enough to remove the need for a control group.

In order to eliminate possible differences due to other variables, age, sex, and educational level were restricted as much as possible. Nine of the ten speakers were women, nine of the ten were in the 20-30 age bracket, and nine of the ten were university students or recent graduates.

Four different types of data were utilized in the analysis: (1) aural transcription of isolated words, (2) palatograms, (3) transcriptions and spectrograms from tapes of isolated words, and (4) transcriptions, spectrograms, and intonation data from tapes of normal conversation.

3. ORIENTAL ISRAELI HEBREW

3.1 /ħ/

The phoneme /ħ/, and its phonetic realization, [ħ] (voiceless pharyngeal fricative), is the most basic feature setting OIH apart from GIH. OIH could, in fact, be called the [ħ]-variety of Israeli Hebrew. It is most basic because it is the only distinguishing characteristic exhibited with total consistency. A true OIH speaker will never give [x] for historical /ħ/. (For a discussion of "intermittent" OIH, see section 4.1 below.)

This maintenance of /ħ/ has a very severe effect on the frequency of [x]. A list of 250 words as recorded by an OIH speaker contained 10 instances of [x] and 34 of [ħ]. This same list recorded by a GIH speaker had 44 occurrences of [x]. Of course, this is to be expected as OIH [x] is merely an allophone of /k/ while GIH [x] is both an allophone of /k/ and the sole realization of the phoneme /x/ (= OIH /ħ/). Still, the listener receives a strong auditory impression of the two varieties of Israeli Hebrew on this basis alone.

Although [ħ] is considered a fricative, it is sometimes articulated with so little friction as to give the impression rather of an approximant. This pronunciation, symbolized as [ħʰ], does not seem conditioned by phonetic environment but is rather typical of the speech of certain individuals, independent of national origin.

3.2 /ʿ/

In contrast to /ħ/, /ʿ/ is no longer maintained consistently by OIH speakers. As in GIH, the most likely realization of historical /ʿ/ is zero. In fact, in an average four minute segment of conversational speech, no more than 35 percent of the occurrences of historical /ʿ/ showed realizations other than [ʾ] or zero. Thus one cannot claim that OIH maintains historical /ʿ/. There is rather an additional possibility of a non-zero phonetic realization of historical /ʿ/ which does not exist for GIH.

When /ʿ/ does have a phonetic realization other than [ʾ] or zero, it can be any one of numerous physical phenomena. These can be divided into two basic categories: (1) [ʿ], that is, some kind of discrete unit and (2) backing of the surrounding vowels.

The published descriptions of [ʿ] in Arabic provide a background for the examination of [ʿ] in OIH. Obrecht (1968:27) reported that Lebanese Arabic [ʿ] is a voiced pharyngeal fricative, showing a rasping onset of irregular and abnormally widely spaced voicing striations. He calls [ʿ] "voiced noise": a harmonic structure plus noise whose formants correspond more or less to those of the following vowel, except for a lowering of the second formant of about 50 msec. in duration. Al-Ani (1970:62-64), in his study of Iraqi Arabic, claims that, while /ʿ/ does take different forms, it is most commonly a voiceless stop.

While OIH apparently exhibits both these types of [ʿ],[4] the most common manifestation is of a different sort entirely: a sometimes laryngealized, voiced approximant or glide having formants roughly in the range of the vowel [a]. OIH [ʿ] seems to be an [a]-type glide in the same sense that [j] is an [i]-type glide.

Figures 1 and 2 provide an illustration. These are spectrograms of the words /ʃivʿim/ 'seventy' and /ʿets/ 'tree'. In both cases, [ʿ] was strongly perceived. The spectrograms indicate that [ʿ] here is voiced, somewhat laryngealized, and a glide, having formants of approximately 730, 1800 and 2600, thus approximately those of the vowel [a]. The formants of the following vowels were unaffected.

As might be expected from this description, [ʿ] in the combination [aʿa] was very difficult to pinpoint. A spectrogram of /taʿam/ 'taste', for example, showed a steady long vowel with laryngealization occurring in the middle. Not surprisingly then, it is precisely in the environment of [a] that a realization of /ʿ/ as a backed vowel is most often observed. Figures 3 and 4 illustrate this phenomenon. Shown here is the classic pair /natati/ 'I gave'

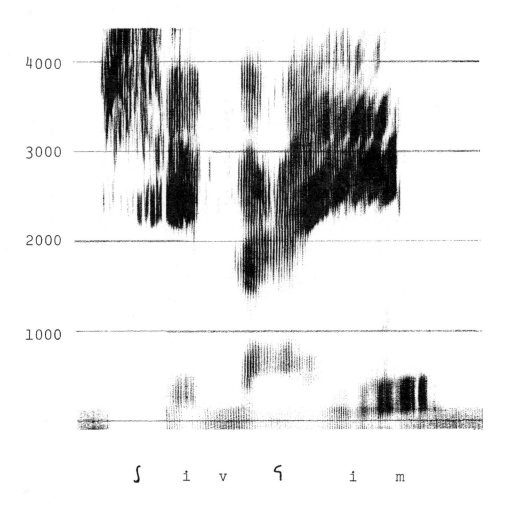

Figure 1. Spectrogram of [ʃivˤim] 'seventy'

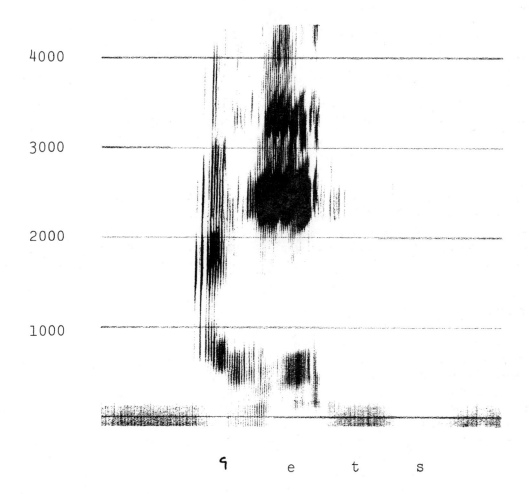

Figure 2. Spectrogram of [ʿêts] 'tree'

and /nataᶜti/ 'I planted'. The former is clearly rendered [natáti], the vowel formants being 710 and 1420. The latter is just as clearly [natá:ti], with formants of 710 and 1170.[5] This can be analyzed as /nataᶜti/ → *[natɑti] → [natá:ti], vowel lengthening due to compensation for the loss of a segment. But compensatory lengthening is not a consistent occurrence. /ᶜ/ may cause backing of a preceding or following vowel, or both, without leaving any trace of an additional segment, e.g. /ʃaᶜatajim/ 'two hours' → [ʃaatájim]. In fact, the opposite may occur. Two vowels which became contiguous due to the loss of /ᶜ/ may further shorten. Thus, one obtains both [pám] and [paˑm] as reflexes of /paᶜam/ 'time, occurrence' (see p. 36, line 9). Finally, vowel backing may co-occur with [ʕ], e.g. [1ᵃᶜɑsot] 'to do', and it may be less severe ([à] rather than [ɑ]).

Taking all these possibilities together, a word like /paᶜam/ may show realizations with /ᶜ/ becoming [ʔ] or zero, with or without additional vowel loss ([páᶜam], [pá:m], [paˑm], [pám]); with /ᶜ/ as [ᶜ], with or without vowel backing ([páᶜam], [páᶜɑm], [pá ᶜɑm]);[6] or with /ᶜ/ as vowel backing, with or without additional vowel loss or lengthening ([pá::m], [pá:m], [páˑm], [pám], [páam], [páa:m]).[6]

The growing inconsistency in the maintenance of /ᶜ/ is demonstrated nicely by cases of hypercorrection among OIH speakers. Since both /ʔ/ and /ᶜ/ frequently show up as zero, they may easily be confused. Zero may be understood as a reflex of /ᶜ/, rather than /ʔ/, and then a more "correct" realization of /ᶜ/ may be utilized. Thus one finds [meᶜá] (/meʔa/ 'hundred'), presumably "rectifying" a normal pronunciation of [meá].

3.3 / r /

OIH and GIH are no longer differentiated by their realizations of /r/. Most speakers of both varieties show a uvular articulation; some speakers of both varieties show a denti-alveolar tap articulation. Thus, all four possible combinations occur. There does seem to be some possible internal communal differentiation. GIH speakers having a denti-alveolar realization of /r/ were frequently associated with Persian origins while OIH speakers having a denti-alveolar realization of /r/ were associated with Yemenite origins. This correlation is, of course, highly tenuous.

3.4 Intonation

Perhaps the single most interesting point of diversion between OIH and GIH is to be found in their respective intonation patterns. This is a subject which has, to my knowledge, never been examined. The study of intonation itself is relatively recent and Israeli Hebrew intonation has hardly begun to be studied. The only work on the subject (Laufer 1977), though well done and clearly presented, is nevertheless an analysis of the speech of one GIH speaker, the author himself. Thus, any statements made about Israeli Hebrew intonation must be taken as highly tentative. And yet Laufer's work can provide a useful point of departure.

Laufer offers a fairly comprehensive view of GIH intonation patterns using a system based largely on that of O'Connor and Arnold (1973) for English. Each "word group", separated off by a pause for breathing or for illustrating syntactic relationships, i.e. paralleling written punctuation, is examined in order to locate three points: (1) the "nucleus", defined as the last stressed syllable of the last important word in the word group; (2) the "head", defined as beginning with the first stressed syllable of the word group and continuing up to the nucleus; and (3) the "pre-head", the collection of unstressed syllables preceding the beginning of the head. Every word group has a nucleus; it may or may not exhibit a head and/or pre-head. The intonation contour is stated in terms of the pitch and pitch changes which occur in these three segments. The nucleus is the syllable in which the main intonation contour is generally executed, while the intonation contours of the head and pre-head add variation and subtlety.

Nine main intonation patterns were found by Laufer. Thus, for example, one GIH contour (Laufer's No. 1) has an optional low-pitched pre-head, an optional low-pitched head, and a small drop in pitch in the nucleus. This is exemplified by the following word group found in the sample text:

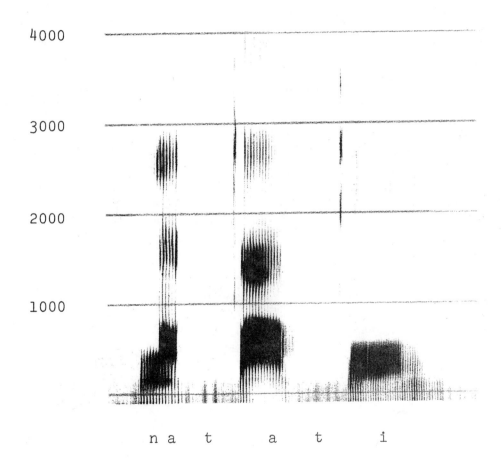

Figure 3. Spectrogram of [natáti] 'I gave'

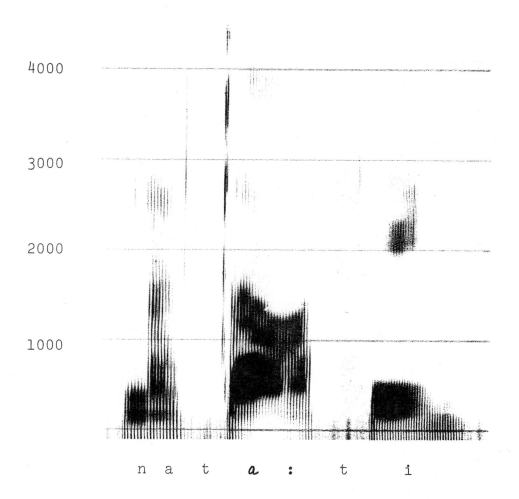

Figure 4. Spectrogram of [natá:ti] 'I planted'

[bî-tel-avîv moxʙim et   zé-ze]

'In-Tel-Aviv they-sell Acc. this-this'
('They   sell   it   in   Tel-Aviv')

The pre-head ([bî-tel-a]) is spoken on a level low pitch; there is no head. The nucleus ([vîv]) shows a small drop to a somewhat lower pitch. The rest of the word group continues on this second, lower level pitch, showing only one stressed syllable, the first [zé].

Besides these nine, certain embellishments known as "emphatic contours" exist. Principally these involve two variations in the shape of the head. One is the "terraced" head, where each successive stressed syllable is on a pitch level higher (in the case of the low-pitched terraced head) or lower (in the case of the high-pitched terraced head) than the preceding group. In other words, while a high-pitched head theoretically shows level pitches (   ), a high-pitched terraced head looks like   , each new level beginning on a stressed syllable. Conversely a normal low-pitched head is like ● · · · while a low-pitched terraced head is rather

It should be noted that this last head is not mentioned in Laufer's book, but is rather a later addition of his. The other variation of the head is the "gliding" head where each syllable is consecutively higher (or lower) than the preceding but each stressed syllable begins a new wave. Thus, a high-pitched gliding head shows up as   while a low-pitched gliding head is conversely   . The high-pitched terraced head is found in the sample text as an illustration:

[ád ʃe-b-a-sóf hu natán li ᵉ-ze bî-meá·]

'until in the end he gave this to me for a hundred...'

It is not possible to discuss the intonation transcription system that has been developed for GIH in full detail nor to review the overall description of GIH intonation that has emerged from Laufer's work. But precisely because his analysis and transcription system were developed for GIH, their applicability to OIH gives some measure of the similarities and differences between them.

When GIH material was transcribed, all went fairly smoothly. The transcription system was adequate to handle most of the intonation contours on the tapes. The transcription of the OIH texts was far more difficult. Often one had the strong feeling of forcing the reality of the taped material into the available transcription system. This was due principally to two factors. First, the OIH speakers "sing" more than the GIH speakers. "Singing" refers to the production of clear, level tones, very much like musical notes. Thus one finds, for example, the sentence [î· ʙatstá lᵒ-otsí bagʙú:t] 'she wanted to complete the baccalaureate' "chanted", the stressed syllables of [ʙatstá] and [lᵒ-otsí] on level high tones and the last stressed syllable of the sentence on a level low tone. Another example of singing can be found in the sample text word [hidvakáĥti] (line 5). A small drop in pitch is marked on the nuclear syllable. But the indication here is not to the expected drop in one syllable (↱) or even a drop over two syllables (●.). Rather each syllable is sung on a level tone, with the second tone on a lower pitch. One is reminded strongly of an operatic "recitatívo". In fact, it was often quite easy to sing along with the tapes.

The second factor causing difficulty in the intonation transcription of OIH material is the inventory of possible contours. As was stated, Laufer found nine main intonation contours in GIH plus certain additional embellishments.

But these do not seem sufficient to cover the range available to the OIH speaker. I refer here not to wholly different contours, but to additional types of variation within the head. As the sample sentences have shown, the pitch sequence of the head is projected to be either level or varied in an extremely systematic way. OIH speakers seem to produce fewer such patterned sequences than do GIH speakers. That is, there are many cases where, while deviation from the expected pitch sequence is not great enough to be classified as something else, it still does not follow the formula. Thus, if GIH speakers produce the "theme" of the piece, then OIH speakers produce the "theme plus variations". For example, consider the following word phrase, [ka'ɾov l-ᴬ-°ᶜatsmᴬ↘ut] 'around Independence (Day)'. The transcription would lead one to reconstruct the phrase as . • • • ↘   . In fact, it was rendered with subtle variation in the head: . • • . ↷   . Another example is the phrase [ʌhi mìsa↘peʙet] 'she tells'. The transcription represents a rendition as • . . ↷   . In actuality, the phrase was said on a pitch sequence of • . • .   . Neither of these head variations fit into the framework of intonation represented by the transcription system.

Finally, significant differences were noted in the frequency of use of some of the main intonation contours. Laufer's contour No. 6, consisting of an optional low-pitched pre-head, an optional low-pitched head, and a small rise in pitch in the nucleus, was approximately twice as common among GIH and "intermittent" OIH (see below) speakers as among OIH speakers. This refers to phrases such as

[mᴬtsánu giná]

. • . ♪

'We found a garden.'

3.5 Miscellaneous features

3.5.1 Consonantal and vocalic length

Consonants which are phonetically longer than others, i.e. articulated over a longer space of time, but not phonologically long were observed numerous times. They occurred with equal frequency in both GIH and OIH data and are transcribed in the sample text (see section 5). Measurements made using spectrograms of these consonants indicated that 200 msec. was the "threshold" for perception of length. While length seems frequently due to hesitation in speech or to emphasis, many instances are unclear as to causation. An earlier, independent report was made of this phenomenon (Blanc 1957a:38), but Blanc also failed to identify a cause.

This same phenomenon can be observed with vowels. In addition, vocalic length may be the result of compensation for the loss of /ᶜ/. This raises the question of the phonemic status of vowel length. Although pairs such as [natáti] (< /natati/ 'I gave') and [natá:ti] (< /nataᶜti/ 'I planted', cf. possible realizations of /ᶜ/, in 3.2) exist, it would seem unwise to claim phonemicity. First of all, one cannot count on the presence of length. /nataᶜti/ is just as likely to be pronounced [natáti]. Secondly, one would be hard put to find such contrasting pairs for any other vowel since the presence of /ᶜ/ conditions the /a/. It would be difficult to claim that /a:/ is the only phonemic long vowel.

3.5.2 Nasalization

Two occurrences of nasalization appear in the sample text, both instances of [ħanũ] (/ħanut/ 'store'). Nasalization in the presence of a nasal consonant is not particularly unusual. However, these two specific examples obscure the fact that nasalization throughout the data seems to occur in the environment of [ħ], not the nasal consonants. Other examples are: [ħõʃév] 'thinks' (occurring twice), [aħʰũz] 'per cent', [ħũts] 'outside', and [bitaħõ·n] 'security'. In the last case, of course, a nasal consonant is also present. It is not at all clear whether all these occurrences should be classed together.

3.5.3 [h]-less speech

The ephemeral nature of [h] has been reported by all observers of GIH from Blanc (1964:136) through Weinberg (1966:65) and Téné (1968:988) to Chayen (1971:692, 1973:25). Chayen's latest description states that [h] varies freely with [ʾ] or zero.

In fact, /h/ is realized as zero in a very great majority of cases by all speakers, both GIH and OIH. The appearance of [ʾ] as a reflex of /h/ was not at all frequent. [h] was found most often when /h/ was initial in a sentence or phrase, i.e. after pause, or when the speed of speech was noticeably slow.

3.5.4 Emphatic consonants

The Semitic "emphatic" consonants, observable in the Hebrew orthography and maintained in spoken Arabic, have disappeared from native Israeli Hebrew, GIH and OIH alike. The phoneme /q/ is realized as [k], falling together with the stop allophone of /k/. The phonemes /ṭ/ and /t/ have merged entirely ([t]). Only /ṣ/ show the pronunciation [ts].

4. INTERMEDIATE VARIETIES

All reports have stated that GIH is spreading while OIH is receding. Not surprisingly, then, intermediate varieties exist. Blanc (1964:135) suggested the likelihood of such intermediate varieties; now this phenomenon can be documented.

4.1 "Intermittent" OIH

Two members of the sample population exhibited "intermittent" OIH. "Intermittent" OIH is defined as the speech of an individual of Middle Eastern background in which [ħ] does appear, but with less than total consistency. In the speech of one person, historical /ħ/ was realized sometimes as [x] and sometimes as [ħ], seemingly at random. The other individual seemed to use [ħ] in social circumstances where she was conscious of her background, and [x] in other social surroundings. While no cases of hypercorrection ([ħ] reflecting /k/) were noted, they undoubtedly occur. Furthermore, as has been noted, these speakers showed a frequency of different intonation contours more like GIH than OIH speakers.

One cannot, of course, speak of the phenomenon of intermediate speech varieties with respect to the maintenance of historical /ʿ/. OIH itself has already become an intermediate variety in this regard.

4.2 "Intermittent" [ɾ]

This type of intermediate variety is not directly correlated with GIH/OIH distinctions. It does involve, however, movement towards a dominant norm. Since uvular articulation is certainly predominant in both sets of speakers (and in particular among speakers of European origins, the "prestige GIH" group) the existence of "intermittent" [ɾ] speech among OIH speakers is not surprising. "Intermittent" [ɾ] speech involves inconsistent utilization of the denti-alveolar [ɾ] versus the uvular [ʁ]. One native Israeli Hebrew speaker of Yemenite background, for instance, showed such varying use of denti-alveolar [ɾ], ranging from 73 percent to 100 percent of all possible occurrences.

This sample did not allow for examination of the possibility of "intermittent" [ɾ] speech among GIH [ɾ]-users. It seems likely that it exists.

5. SAMPLE TEXT

The speaker, S. S., is a 29-year-old woman whose grandparents immigrated to Israel from Iraq. The text is given in phonetic transcription, with intonation transcription, and in English translation.

A caret, marked sideways, is used to denote backing, e.g. [ė] , a vowel between [e] and [ə] , or [ȯ] , a particularly back [o] , or fronting, e.g. [ó] , a vowel between [o] and [ə] . Openness is indicated by a hook under the vowel symbol, e.g. [e̦] , a position between [e] and [ɛ] , while closeness is indicated by a hook above the vowel symbol, e.g. [ǎ] , a position between [a] and [ʌ] . Raised symbols are used to show very rapid articulation. A raised reversed stress symbol (ˋ) shows secondary stress. ˙, :, and :: specify three variations in length.

1   vé :: kàníti gám et^h-a-tík ha-zé :...avᴧl zé bⁱ -iʁ-a-atiká.
2   zé bⁱ -iʁ-a-atiká vᵃl jéʃ od aʁ.bé:, gám be̦ :...bì -tel-aví v
3   moxʁim et zé-ze, ze meá-v^-mǎla líʁot. ze noʁá jaká: (ʁ.)¹
4   hu ʁatsá meá-ʃivim líʁot u ʁatsá vᵃ-aní ko-káx:
5   hìdvakáh̄ti² vⁱ-h̄ìtkotátì . ʃaatáji̇m jaʃáfti b-a-h̄anú̃(t)³ .
6   lámǎ aní oléxet, u koʁé li bi-h̄azaʁá. aní oléxet, u-
7   koʁé-li. tóv-àz⁴ k-ʃg̦-u-koʁe̦, ᵃnᵃh̄nu⁵ midvakh̄ím ve-zé
8   b-a-sóf nigmáʁ ʃálðm! ȯd h̄ǎ-páˤam, tȯv bói bói ᵃní oʁíd-
9   la⁶ . vi-kól pa˙m kól pam⁷ kǎ-xá ʃaatáji̇m jaʃáfti b-a-
10 h̄anú̃, ád ʃe-b-a-sóf hu natán li ᵉ-ze bì -meá ʃloʃím
11 lí ʁot ʃté-tikim. ʃté tikím meá-ʃlˠ⁰ àvál (...) ʃa:táji̇m.
12 v-ze ló kᵊ-xa...ǎz:ᵃ b-a-sóf lakáh̄ ti-ᵉ-ze jéʃ ód-eh̄ad
13 má-ʃᵊ-u gám jaʃé mìȭd, vé:ᵐ...kànìtì:...mǎ od kàníti kámà
14 dvaʁ ím gám kén. á hají̇ti be-kól-bo ʃǎlóm. kàníti
15 h̄ultsót totséʁet h̄úts, ʃ-em b-emét jafótˢ⁸.aʁnél ka-zé̦.

¹   No [ʁ] is heard but one does hear a slight constriction in the back of the mouth.
²   Voicing assimilation, from /hitvakah̄ti/.
³   No final [t] was heard but, since the speaker clapped her hands at this moment, it is impossible to know whether or not it was articulated. Cf., however, line 10. Loss of a final consonant is a fairly frequent phenomenon. For nasalization, see section 3.5.2 above.
⁴   The [z] quickly devoices to [s] .
⁵   The [n] closure is not complete.
⁶   /lax/.
⁷   For a discussion of the variant forms of /paˤam/ in the text, see section 3.2.
⁸   Forceful articulation of word-final [t], as here with slight affrication, was noticed at one time or another among all the women of the sample. Discussion with them yielded the opinion that this is an affectation of speech common among young women who consider themselves sophisticated.

For the intonation transcription, each word group is set off by a vertical line. Within the text of the word group itself, several symbols are utilized. Low-pitched pre-heads are unmarked, while high-pitched pre-heads are indicated by a horizontal line placed high in front of the first syllable of the pre-head. A low-pitched head is marked by a vertical line placed low in front of the first syllable of the head while a high-pitched head uses a similar mark placed high. The same mark, but repeated before each stressed syllable of the head, indicates a high- or low-pitched terraced head, depending on the placement of the mark. Arrows are used to designate gliding heads.

The nuclear intonation contour is transcribed as follows. A small drop in pitch is indicated before the nucleus as ˎ, a large drop as ˋ, a small rise as ˏ, and a large rise as ˊ. A rise followed by a fall is marked ᴧ , while a fall followed by a rise is marked ˇ . Other stressed syllables in the head or the "tail" (what remains after the nucleus) are marked by open circles, high or low depending on their pitch.

Finally, it should be noted that level nuclear tones are marked ⊥ (high or low indicating pitch). This symbol is not used by Laufer, but is rather the addition of the investigator.

1   ⊥ve::│ kàˈniti °gam etʰ-a-°tik ha-ˇze:.│ avˆlˈze bⁱ-iʁ-a-ati⊥ka│

2   ‚ze bⁱ-iʁ-a-ati⊥ka│ vᵃlˈjeʃ od aʁɓe:│ ˈgam⊥bẹ:.│ bi-tel-a⌐viv

3   moxʁim et ₒze-ze│ ze me‚a-vˆ-°mala ˇliʁot│ ze noˈʁa ja ˇka: (ʁ)│

4   hu ʁaˈtsa me°a-ʃivim ˇliʁot u ʁaₒtsa│ vᵃ-aˇni ko-⊥kax:│

5   ˇhidva⌐kaħti│ vⁱ-ˌhitkó̇tati│ ʃaaˈtajⁱm ja°ʃafti b-a-ħa⌐nũ̇(t)│

6   ⌐laₒma│ aˇni ₒₒlexet│ u koₗʁe li bⁱ-ħaza⌐ʁa│ aˇni ₒₒlexet│ u-

7   ko⌐ʁe-li│ ⌐tov-àz│ ˇk·ʃ₂̇-u-kó̇ ʁẹ│ aⁿaħnu midvakˇhim ve-ₒze│

8   b-a-⊥sof│ nig⊥maʁ│ ˇʃalom!│ ₗod hᵃ̇-paᶜam│ ˈtov°boiˈboi aᵒni o⌐ʁid-

9   la│ vi-ˇkòl paˑm│ ˇkol pɑm kà̇-ₒxa│ ʃaᵃtajⁱm ja°ʃafti b-a-

10 ha ˆnũ̇│ ˈad ʃe-b-a-ˈsof hu naˈtan li ᵉ-ze bⁱ-me ˆa·│ ʃloˈʃim

11 ⌐liʁot│ ⌐ʃte-tikim│ ˇʃte tiˇkim me⊥-a-ʃlᵒ│ a⊥val (...)│ ʃa:ˇtajⁱm│

12 v-ze ⌐lo kᵊ-xa│ ⌐az:ᵃ│ b-a-ˈsof la⌐kaħti-ᵉ-ze│ ˈjeʃ ⌐od-eħad│

13 ˈma-ʃᵊ-u°gam ja°fe mⁱ-ᵒ̇d│ ⊥ve:ᵐ..│ ˈkà̇⊥niti:.│ ⌐ma od│ kà̇ˈniti ˈkamà̇

14 dvaˈʁim ⌐gam ₒken│ ⊥a│ haˈjiti be-°kol-bo ʃà̇ lom│ kà̇ˇniti

15 hulˇtsot toˇtseʁet ⌐huts│ ʃ-em b-eˈmet ja⌐fotˢ..│ aʁ⌐nel ka-ₒze│

Line 1, word group 2: The drop in pitch starts from a high point but falls only part-way to the bottom of the range.

Line 3, word group 1: As Laufer notes (1977:29), a low-pitched head before a large drop in pitch is not ● ● ● ⌐ but rather ● · ˙ ⌐ . For this reason, the stressed syllable in [°mala] is marked high.

Line 3, word group 2: The drop here is exceedingly slow and long.

Line 4, last word group and line 5, word groups 1 and 2: This entire sentence is rendered in a typically OIH singing style with considerable variation of pitch within the head.

Line 8, word groups 1, 2, and 3: All three phrases present the distinctive singing style.

The line numbers of the translation follow those of the text. Parentheses are used for additions to the text necessitated by English.

1   And...I bought this bag too, but this (was) in the Old City.[1]
2   This was in the Old City, but there are many more (like it), also in...in Tel-Aviv
3   they sell it, it's, it's a hundred pounds[2] and up. It's awfully expensive.
4   He wanted 170 pounds, he did, and I
5   argued and bickered so much. I spent two hours in the store!
6   Why? I leave, he calls me back. I leave, he
7   calls me. O.K., so when he calls, we argue and so,
8   in the end it's over, good-bye! Once again, O.K. come, come, I'll lower (the price)
9   for you.[3] And every time, every time like this two hours I spent in the
10 store, until in the end he gave this to me for 130
11 pounds—two bags. Two bags, a hundred and thir..., but two hours.

12   And it's not so...So in the end I took this one. There's another one,
13   also something very nice, and...I bought...what else? I bought some
14   things, too. Ah, I was at the Shalom Department Store.[4] I bought
15   foreign-made blouses that are really nice—sort of Arnel.

---

[1] The ancient walled city of Jerusalem.

[2] She is referring to the price in Israeli pounds.

[3] Here she is speaking as the store proprietor.

[4] "Department Store" is expressed by the phrase "everything in it".

6. CONCLUSION

Movement is apparently still uni-directional, from OIH to GIH. "Intermittent" OIH speakers are the best evidence of this. The continued official advocacy of OIH, such as its required use by radio announcers, seems to have had absolutely no effect. Even in its strictest sense, OIH seems to be more similar to GIH now than it was in the early 60's. While this precise description of OIH now requires validation over a larger sample of speakers, particularly in the areas of educational and socio-economic levels, the question must be asked: what is to become of OIH? Are there any social factors operating to prevent OIH loss?

A very preliminary look into the subject pointed up two factors. The first was the ethnic mixture of the elementary and high schools attended. (The make-up of the speaker's residential neighborhood did not seem to have any effect.) The second factor is the psychological attitude of the speaker towards being "Oriental". Furthermore, the two factors seemed to interact. Those individuals of Oriental background who attended schools with predominantly Middle Eastern and North African populations generally emerged as OIH speakers. Half of those who attended schools with students from predominantly European homes became OIH speakers and the other half, GIH speakers. The ultimate choice seemed to correlate with the individual's attitude towards himself/herself as "Oriental". One family is particularly interesting in this regard. There are six children in the family (of Iraqi origin), each of whom attended a different school. In five out of six cases, there was direct agreement between the variety spoken and the type of schooling received. The sixth child speaks GIH "in spite of" attending a predominantly Middle Eastern school. He had mostly European friends in school and identified with them.

Thus, barring a strong movement of identification with their heritage from within the Oriental communities themselves, and given the current social and educational structure in Israel, it seems that OIH is headed for extinction, at least at the educated levels of society. We may be witnessing a process by which an originally geographically-based speech variety turns into a socio-economically defined one.

FOOTNOTES

[1] This paper has been adapted from the doctoral dissertation, "The phonetics of Israeli Hebrew: 'Oriental' versus 'General' Israeli Hebrew", accepted for the Ph.D. degree by UCLA in September 1978. The work was made possible through the generosity of the Jewish Federation-Council of Greater Los Angeles, the Government of Israel, and the United States-Israel Educational Foundation. Many thanks are due to Dr. Wolf Leslau, under whose direction the work was done, to Dr. Peter Ladefoged, and to Dr. Asher Laufer for the use of the Phonetics Laboratory at the Hebrew University.

[2] Blanc actually used the term "Arabicized Israeli". This term is not used here because it seems to imply (though Blanc denies this) that the Hebrew of the speaker has been made to conform to the patterns of Arabic. While this is possible, there is certainly no proof for it.

[3] The most extensive work on the subject (Chayen 1973) treats "Educated Israeli Hebrew". According to the author, this is identical to Blanc's "General Israeli". Furthermore, Chayen (1971:692, 1973:25) questions the existence of OIH among educated individuals, even near-natively. He states that he found [ħ] in the speech of only three or four (out of approximately 150) university students whom he studied. These had already had two or three years of secondary schooling in Arabic-speaking countries before immigrating to Israel.

[4] While this author did not find any non-glide occurrences of [ʕ], Laufer and Condax (1978, personal communication) have demonstrated their existence among OIH speakers. Their work on the articulatory basis of [ʕ] portrays the set of possible articulations—stop, fricative, glide—as a "strong" to "weak" spectrum of [ʕ] pronunciation. Their data was derived from a study of [ʕ] in isolation, in isolated words, with mechanical aids, and with the total awareness of the subject as to what was being studied. The data under discussion here is extremely casual speech. This probably explains the preference for glide [ʕ] in this author's data and the preference for stop [ʕ] in their work.

[5] Morag (1967:643) makes the claim that many GIH speakers show [a] while OIH speakers do not. His premise is that /ʕ/ is realized as [ʕ] in OIH and often as [a] in GIH. That OIH speakers certainly do possess [a] is, it seems, proven quite conclusively. The matter is more difficult as regards GIH speakers. No occurrence of [a] was found among the GIH speakers in the sample. /nataʕ ti/ was invariably rendered either as [natáti] (i.e. identical to /natati/) or as [natá·ti] with a somewhat longer vowel. However, Morag only claims that some GIH speakers have [a]. It is possible that by chance this sample did not include them.

[6] /ʕ/ seems to affect the following /a/ or both /a/, but not the preceding one alone. When the following vowel was other than /a/, this did occur, e.g. [tsaʕíʁ]   < /caʕir/ 'young'.

BIBLIOGRAPHY

Al-Ani, S.   1970.   *Arabic Phonology; an acoustical and physiological investigation.* The Hague: Mouton.

Blanc, H.   1957a.   "Keta shel dibur ivri yisraeli." [A passage of Israeli Hebrew speech] *Leshonenu* 21:33-39.

————.   1957b.   "Hebrew in Israel: Trends and problems." *Middle East Journal* 11:397-409.

————.   1964.   "Israeli Hebrew texts." *Studies in Egyptology and Linguistics in honour of H. J. Polotsky,* pp. 132-152. Jerusalem: Israel Exploration Society.

————.   1973.   "Israeli Hebrew in perspective." *Ariel* 32:93-104.

Chayen, M.   1971.   "Restructuring of phonetic rules in Modern Hebrew." *International Congress of Phonetic Sciences* 7:691-694.

————.   1973.   *The Phonetics of Modern Hebrew.* The Hague: Mouton.

Devens, M.   1978.   "The Phonetics of Israeli Hebrew: 'Oriental' versus 'General' Israeli Hebrew." Doctoral dissertation, UCLA.

Laufer, A.   1977.   *Hangana shel ivrit meduberet* [The intonation of spoken Hebrew]. Jerusalem: The Hebrew University Press.

Laufer, A. and I. Condax   1978. "Pharyngeal articulation." Personal communication.

Morag, S.   1959.   "Planned and unplanned development in Modern Hebrew." *Lingua* 8:247-263.

————.   1967.   "Uniformity and diversity in a language: dialects and forms of speech in Modern Hebrew." *Tenth International Congress of Linguists* 1:639-644.

————.   1972-73.   "Hearot axadot le-teura shel maarexet ha-tnuot shel ha-ivrit ha-meduberet be-yisrael [Some remarks concerning the description of the vocalic system of spoken Israeli Hebrew]." *Leshonenu* 37:205-214.

Obrecht, D.   1968.   *Effects of the Second Formant on the Perception of Velarization Consonants in Arabic.* The Hague: Mouton.

O'Connor, J. D. and G. F. Arnold   1973. *Intonation of Colloquial English,* 2nd ed. London: Longmans.

Téné, D.   1968.   "L'hébreu contemporain." *Le Langage,* pp. 975-1002. Ed. A. Martinet. Paris: Editions Gallimard.

Weinberg, W. 1966.   "Spoken Israeli Hebrew: trends in the departures from classical phonology." *Journal of Semitic Studies* 11:40-68.